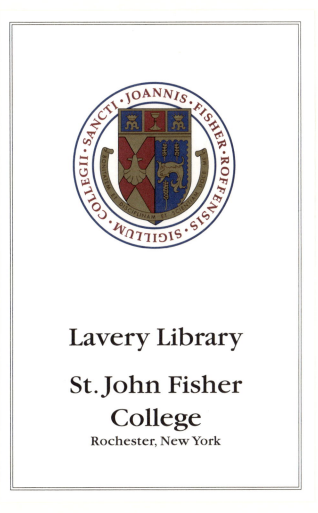

Lavery Library

St. John Fisher
College
Rochester, New York

MONEY MAKES US RELATIVES

Woman hired to clean a middle-class home.

MONEY MAKES US RELATIVES:
Women's Labor in Urban Turkey

Jenny B. White

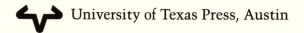 University of Texas Press, Austin

First edition, 1994

Requests for permission to reproduce material from this work
should be sent to Permissions, University of Texas Press, Box 7819,
Austin, TX 78713-7819.

ⓧ The paper used in this publication meets the minimum requirements of American National Standard for Information Sciences—Per-
manence of Paper for Printed Library Materials, ANSI Z39.48-1984.

Library of Congress Cataloging-in-Publication Data
White, Jenny B. (Jenny Barbara), date
    Money makes us relatives : women's labor in urban Turkey / by
Jenny B. White. — 1st ed.
        p.   cm.
    Includes bibliographical references and index.
    ISBN 0-292-79077-5. — ISBN 0-292-79086-4 (pbk.)
    1. Women—Employment—Turkey—Istanbul. 2. Rural-urban
migration—Turkey—Istanbul. 3. Households—Turkey—
Istanbul. 4. Home labor—Turkey—Istanbul. 5. Piece-work—
Turkey—Istanbul. 6. Women—Turkey—Istanbul—Social
conditions. I. Title.
HD6181.93.W48   1994
331.4'09561—dc20   93-30881

To my parents

Contents

Preface

Unless one elects to create artificial boundaries—by studying one particular neighborhood, for instance—anthropological fieldwork in a large urban area can seem like counting grains of sand on a beach. Whenever one looks up from the particular task at hand, new vistas present themselves to be explored. Any description of the large and varied populations of cities must be the province of sampling and statistical extrapolation. Although this book is based on observations in many areas of Istanbul, it makes no attempt to represent either Turkish culture as a whole or Turkish urban culture. Rather, it is an attempt to make visible certain interconnections within the lives of urban dwellers who share characteristics of gender and class and who participate in some form of small-scale commodity production. Its project is to seek regularities within a variety of urban behavior, patterns in the sand that express the complex interactions of an environment's basic elements and that therefore can be found repeated on a number of different scales.

Just as any boundaries that I would draw in a city to define populations or communities would be artificial, structures and patterns discovered and observed in particular social contexts also are limited by the definition of that context. For instance, studies of exchange in marriage, a woman's life cycle in the family, or women's homework, while giving insight into those aspects of social life, restrict speculation to within the boundaries of their subject matter. These run the risk of becoming conceptual boundaries as well. In this book I shift the focus away from discrete relations between individuals and between defined groups to a web of simultaneous, multiple relations. I emphasize the interconnectedness of daily practice.

New conceptual tools are needed to represent such levels of complexity, while still being able to abstract dyadic and intergroup relations within specific contexts. Mutual indebtedness is one useful concept for understanding multiple relations within a group. During my fieldwork I quickly became aware that people tried to keep relations open-ended through the creation and maintenance of indebtedness. Mutual indebtedness provided the foundation for group membership and solidarity, whether that group was the family or a community of tradesmen. While the indebting interaction often took place between individuals, the entire group was a resource from which assistance was available. This assistance generally was asked of another individual, but not in reference to any particular debt owed by that individual and thereby "closed" through payment, but rather in an appeal to a diffuse, generalized reciprocal indebtedness that identified each individual as a member of the group or community. In other words, the exchange of debts is one pattern which characterizes complex group relations and which can be traced in the relations between discrete individuals and groups.

This book is based on two years of anthropological fieldwork in Istanbul, Turkey, among peasant families who have migrated to the city and live in what generally are referred to as squatter (*gecekondu*) districts and in poor working-class neighborhoods. The distinction between squatter areas and poor working-class neighborhoods in Istanbul can no longer be distinctly drawn. While the majority of the population of the various neighborhoods I visited has migrated from the countryside (as has over 60 percent of the population of Istanbul as a whole), the neighborhoods themselves generally (though not all) are integrated structurally into urban metropolitan life. Thus these neighborhoods, like other urban neighborhoods, are characterized by a multiplicity of economic activities ranging from merchandising to individual production in the home.

I observed over a period of two years a number of families engaged in small-scale production. I also conducted interviews with homeworkers, piecework distributors, intermediaries, and families owning their own ateliers in various districts of Istanbul, as well as with merchants, exporters, and government representatives. This discussion refers specifically to a population of women who have migrated from rural areas to Istanbul and who live in communities characterized by low income, poor though generally extant infrastructure, and a mixture of legally and illegally built housing. I contrast the observations I made in squatter districts and other poor neighborhoods with information obtained from merchant-class, middle-class, and educated urbanites, with media accounts, and with other published materials.

Since I had lived in Ankara for three years in the 1970's and had attended university there, my reentry into Turkish society was greatly facilitated. In fact, when I arrived to do my fieldwork I was presented with an ethnographer's dream—a large number of social connections. My close friends brought me into the homes of their working-class relatives and friends, so I was able to enter these communities as trusted "fictional kin" rather than as an outsider. To state this in terms of the thesis of this book, many years of reciprocal indebtedness has provided me with access to a rich variety of "social webs."

Other kind people took me to visit their friends and relatives who did piecework or owned or worked in ateliers. Unless a particular rapport developed, I generally visited these families or ateliers only once or twice. I interviewed the owners, both husband and wife, and, if possible, the workers, using an open-ended interview schedule which ensured that comparable information was obtained about the functioning of the atelier or the piecework arrangements, and about people's attitudes toward their work. However, I was always ready to chat over tea, and some of the most enlightening information came during such conversations. With several families I developed close relations and spent extended periods of time in their homes over the two-year research period.

It is difficult to give a meaningful figure of the dozens of families I visited and interviewed. Some I visited very often, others only once. Some are old friends, others new acquaintances. Several friends are among the educated elite, others are merchants, workers, or housewives with only a basic education. They range in age from twenty-five to sixty-five. I discussed many of my evolving ideas with them and owe them a great debt for their patience in listening to my questions and in explaining what to them probably seemed self-evident. I also appreciate their honesty in telling me when I was on the wrong track.

With regard to organized production sites, I observed in detail ten family ateliers and piecework enterprises in various parts of Istanbul. I observed many more in a more superficial manner, whenever I had the opportunity, asking questions without the formality of an introduction or an interview.

In addition to my observations of workers and atelier owners, I conducted formal interviews with two large-scale exporters of products manufactured through subcontracting and through piecework, and with the manager of an export cooperative. I also interviewed government, bank, and private development foundation officials about the distribution and organization of family labor and small industry, the extent of subcontracting, policies regarding squatter settlements, credit opportunities, and cooperative activities.

Despite the protestations of the women doing piecework that they were "not working," I felt that their labor was being exploited by the class of merchants, intermediaries, and exporters who profited most from the sale of the products they made. I wanted to find a way to improve their situation and, for this reason, approached a private development foundation with a proposal for setting up women's co-operatives in Turkish cities. These cooperative ventures would provide the women with direct access to the export market and would eliminate the intermediary, thus increasing the amount of money the women received for their labor. Although the foundation director expressed interest in the project and acknowledged the need for such an undertaking, lack of funds prevented its implementation.

Several months later, I attended a conference on Islamic banking held at Marmara University, the theme of which was the potential of Islamic banks for providing small Turkish businesses with venture capital. Both venture capital and Islamic banking are based on similar principles of sharing profit and sharing loss, rather than charging interest. This seemed to me also a suitable venue for providing small loans to poor men and women with no collateral who wanted to start or expand a small business, but who did not have the growth potential generally preferred by suppliers of venture capital. Small loans to the poor have been very successful in alleviating poverty and exploitative labor situations in other parts of the world, notably in Bangladesh through the Grameen Bank.

I pursued this funding source, first discussing the feasibility of such a project with an expert on Islamic banking at the Islamic Conference Organization in Ankara, then proposing the idea to a representative of Al Baraka, an Islamic bank that had recently opened a branch in Turkey. In its brochure, the Al Baraka Bank lists its first objective as being "to secure an economic and financial system based on mutual cooperation which is directed towards the prosperity of the society in conformity with the principles of justice and benevolence." Mutual cooperation, benevolence, justice, and no-interest loans were exactly what was needed in the poor neighborhoods of Istanbul.

However, Al Baraka Bank, like any other bank, was interested in large accounts. The bank representative was apologetic and said that, although loans to the poor did seem a suitable activity for an Islamic bank, their hands were tied because they had to operate within a competitive capitalist context.

While I am disappointed that I was unable to help alleviate the exploitative characteristics of piecework as it is structured in Istanbul at the moment, I hope that by documenting the labor process, I have at least contributed to the effectiveness of any future attempts at alternative organization of Turkish urban working-class women's labor.

Acknowledgments

This book would not have been possible without the generosity and encouragement of many friends and colleagues. In particular, I would like to thank Robert Fernea, my advising professor at the University of Texas at Austin, for his intellectual guidance and generous sharing of ideas. He set many of the signposts leading me to this book, although he cannot be held accountable for the journey I have elected to take within. I am grateful to James Brow for his encouragement, tolerance, and gentle direction and to Richard Adams for his constructive challenge of my ideas and his unswerving support. Ira Buchler's sense of humor and proportion helped me through the difficult periods of returning from the field and writing. I owe a particular debt of thanks to Elizabeth Warnock Fernea for her encouragement, support, and inspiration in every way: in writing, in teaching, in thinking through the ideas on which this work is based. Akile Gürsoy Tezcan has been a pillar of strength and inspiration, providing friendship, assistance, an invaluable exchange of ideas, and the example of her own work and compassion for the women she encounters.

I would also like to thank Henry Selby, Laura Lein, Carol Delaney, Barbara Kellner-Heinkele, Ayşe Çağlar, and Clement Henry for their careful reading of the manuscript. I benefited greatly from exchanges with a fellow anthropologist in Turkey, Belkıs Üşümezsoy Kümbetoğlu. Her friendship, assistance, advice, and criticism made my research both better and more enjoyable. Laurie Graham and T. M. Scruggs helped to edit portions of the manuscript and provided regular doses of encouragement. My many friends in Austin gave me a great deal of moral support and salutary distraction. I would also like to thank Susan Lane for her patience and concern and the staff of the Center for Middle Eastern Studies, particularly Ian Manners, Marjorie Payne, Annes McCann-Baker, Diane Watts, Cora Boyett,

Dolly Robinson, Virginia Howell, and Deborah Littrell, for making a home for me these many years.

Funding for my research was provided by grants from Fulbright-Hays and the National Science Foundation. The University of Texas Center for Middle Eastern Studies and the Institute of Turkish Studies, Inc., also assisted my studies. I am grateful for this institutional support. Neither these institutions nor my friends and colleagues, however, are responsible for the ideas expressed here.

The success of this project is owed primarily to the Turkish families that opened their homes and their lives to me. I appreciate their hospitality and their friendship.

Jenny B. White

MONEY MAKES US RELATIVES

Women knitting at a neighbor's home.

Women buying cloth from an itinerant vendor.

Chapter 1
Introduction

"Turkey is like a bus headed West with all the passengers
running East."   —An Istanbul taxi driver

Seher picked up a sweater she was knitting. The little girls picked
up some knitting also, and suddenly I was surrounded by what
seemed like dozens of long silver needles flashing in the air, as if in
a field of crickets. Up and down, up and down the needles went. The
unison lasted only a few minutes before someone dropped her knitting on the couch and got up, leaving it there. Someone else may
come along later, find it and knit a few rows. The whole process of
knitting seems random and, like breathing, unconscious. In the
working-class neighborhoods of urban Turkey the assumption is
that any woman can do such handiwork, and that the skill is therefore nothing special. In fact, a woman as wife is in part *defined* by
such abilities. Women's identity as family members is constructed
from childhood around such labor and duty to kin.

In recent years the skills and labor that are "natural" to women's
role and identity have increasingly been put to use in the small-scale
production of commodities. In the following chapters I will link the
enactment through labor of women's identity within the family to
Turkish urban working-class women's production for the national
and international market. The aim of this book, the result of two
years' fieldwork in Istanbul, is to bring to light the ideology that
underlies power relations in small-scale commodity production in
urban Turkey. Since much of this production is aimed at the world
market, what is revealed is not only a syncretism of capitalism and
local culture but also a basic mechanism by which international
business takes advantage of the cultural construction of labor and of
the production process to create a pool of cheap, expendable, primarily female labor.

The descriptions presented here of the productive lives of urban

Turkish women and of the production process in which they participate lead to a critique of theories of small-scale production that do not adequately take into account kinship and the notions of gender, hierarchy, and obligation which it incorporates. The centrality of bonds of kinship, family, and community in women's productive lives in general and in their commodity-producing activities in particular challenges ideas about the necessity of conflict between exploiter and exploited assumed in much theory dealing with production under capitalism.

While the extraction of profit from unpaid or poorly paid women's labor is, at one remove, clearly exploitative,[1] there is a positive aspect to the women's productive activities beyond any immediate monetary return. Through the production process they participate in relations of reciprocity which strengthen social bonds and reiterate their membership in important social groups. Such groups as the family and community form the bulwark of these women's long-term social and economic security.

The structure of hierarchy and domination in the patriarchal family and the requirements of reciprocity inherent in kinship provide a metaphor for the euphemization of exploitative relations within these specifically capitalist forms of small-scale commodity production. In other words, the exploitation of labor is also a means to social solidarity. In the following chapters, I will construct a moral economy of capitalist small enterprise in urban Turkey, within which the exchange of labor for money is represented as reciprocity characteristic of kinship.

The economic consequences of how women define and express themselves became clear to me slowly over a cumulative period of five years when I lived first in Ankara, the capital, between 1975 and 1978, then Istanbul, the largest city, between 1986 and 1988. Over this long stretch of time I was initiated into and became practiced at fulfilling the requirements of long-term relationships in this society. I am now at the center of my own web of relationships with their accompanying duties, debts, and benefits, and I have learned both the limits that these relationships impose on my behavior and the joy and security to be derived from them. The entwining of lives this entails creates a sturdy and reliable basis for a particular kind of growth, like that of a tree, each interaction forcing sustenance through the trunk into limbs and blossoms. All available energy is absorbed by a limiting but enduring and reliable social form.

During my last visit, between 1986 and 1988, to conduct field research on women's small-scale commodity production in Istanbul squatter districts, I noticed an enormous difference in the economic environment since the 1970's, brought about by the Özal government's free-market policies.[2] I was also struck by the ubiquitousness of piecework. As in the course of my research I sought out and came to know working-class women involved in home production or working in family ateliers, I understood that what to me seemed a new activity in response to intensified financial need and opened markets, these women explained as a branching of their traditional activities and relationships, as if the tree had grown another limb producing the same blossoms.

From a distance, however, the context is different; the profits of intermediaries and exporters can be calculated against the women's wages, and the products can be observed at the final stage of their travels, sold abroad at many times their production cost. From this distance, the new branch seems more a graft than a naturally occurring extension of the tree itself. This book is an attempt to combine the view at each distance in order to gain a clearer understanding of the functioning of such *trompe l'oeil* capitalism.

Part 1 provides a brief overview of Istanbul's mixed ideological heritage and of the city's growth. Both are important for understanding the pressures and contradictions that characterize today's urban culture. Part 2 describes the constitution of the working-class female subject within that culture and the discourse within which women learn to be women and learn to labor. In Part 3 gender, identity, and obligation are drawn together in a finely grained description of small-scale piecework production.

The final chapter directs this evidence of the importance of ideology within the production process at Marxist theories of small-scale commodity production. While theorists have of late acknowledged the importance of such factors as kinship, patriarchy, and gender relations within the petty-commodity-producing household, they have stopped short of incorporating such ideological and political factors into their theories of petty production itself, preferring to see relations within the family or household as noncapitalist, albeit important, influences on household members' capitalist production.

This blindness to the centrality of social relations to the production process itself is due in part to the antagonistic dualism between wage labor and capital which forms the bedrock of Marxist economic theory. Since, it is argued, commodity-producing household members both own the means of production and are the producers, the conflict between capital and labor traditionally at the base of capitalist activity is not present. Therefore relations within the household cannot in themselves be capitalist relations.

The weight of evidence accumulated in this study shows that

while small-scale production in Turkey is indeed capitalist production, the relations within the production process can also be capitalist relations, euphemized as kinship. That is, the relations of production can be at one and the same time exploitative and solidary. This is true whether production takes place within the household or in a workshop.

Distinguishing power relations within the commodity-producing family as also being capitalist relations of exploitation is an important and necessary step toward understanding the role of gender and kinship ideology in constructing a system of labor and production for the world market. Without this step the family remains a noncapitalist black box connected to its capitalist context by virtue of its class position and participation in the market.

Labor as Leisure

In recent years a specialized global economy has emerged that takes advantage of pools of cheap labor in less prosperous countries either by transferring labor-intensive production from industrialized to less industrialized countries, by subcontracting labor in these countries, or through advantages accrued from the resale of cheaply produced products.

International subcontracting has become firmly rooted economically as well as conceptually in many Western countries. In Germany, the term *Billiglohnländer* (cheap-wage countries) has wide currency even among the German working class. Increasing use of this word in Germany coincides with declining interest in home knitting; in the past eight years imported hand-knitted sweaters, which sell for prices lower than the equivalent domestic cost of wool, have flooded the German market. Many of these sweaters and other clothing items in Europe and the United States are imported from Turkey, where they are produced primarily by women and children within a system of piecework labor and in small family ateliers.

The concentration of women in piecework and atelier production that is oriented toward both the local and international markets is not limited to Turkey. Benería and Roldán show a similar phenomenon in their study of industrial homework and subcontracting in Mexico City, which exposes the links between women's work and "global processes whose center of gravity is at the higher level of the subcontracting pyramid" (1987:166). In Narsapur, India, lace destined for export is produced exclusively by women who work from their homes (Mies 1982).

In each of these cases, the women and the (largely male) organizers of their labor perceive the women's production activities as being part of their gendered domesticity, rather than as productive work under capitalist conditions. This denial is an attempt to consolidate work for pay not only with family duties, but also with the requirements of gender identity. Both are characteristics common to systems of small-scale production using female labor.

Çinar notes, for example, in her 1987 surveys of female homeworkers in urban Turkey, that the women in her samples work an average of twenty-two hours a week and have been homeworkers for an average of four years (1989, 1991). Nevertheless, none of the women "took their work seriously or considered themselves as working" (1989:15). In another example, women provide the labor for the primarily home-based Turkish carpet-weaving industry. Weaving, however, is interpreted by the weavers, their male kin, and by census enumerators as a leisure activity, even where it is a full-time occupation (Berik 1987).

Similarly, in Mexico, although the traditional opposition to married women's paid work has decreased, women industrial homeworkers in Mexico City still reevaluate "a remunerated working role within the definition of 'proper' motherhood" (Benería and Roldán 1987:142). In Narsapur poor, secluded Christian and Hindu women often spend six to eight hours a day producing lace which reaches the world market through a network of male agents but consider themselves to be housewives, rather than workers (Mies 1982; see also the collection of articles on women in home-based production in Singh and Kelles-Viitanen 1987).

Until recently, analyses of small-scale commodity production have tended to emphasize the economic determinants of its structure, using either a Marxist framework that focuses on the study of modes of production and their articulation (Kahn 1978, 1980; A. Scott 1979) or a dualistic framework, in which the economic activities of the poor are localized as an informal or marginal sector in opposition to a formal or dominant sector of the economy. Neither orientation has been able to present a satisfactory account of the complexity of small-scale production in fully capitalist and mixed capitalist economies. A number of studies, for example, point to the artificiality of the formal/informal division and argue that the sectors are mutually dependent and highly integrated.[3]

Structural Marxist analyses have been hampered by an overemphasis on the economic. Chevalier (1983) and Smith (1984a, 1984b) have attempted to rectify this by including ideological and political as well as economic factors in their analyses. This broader consideration opens the door to studies of the development of diversity *within* the sector of small production (see, for example, Smith 1986; Friedmann 1986).

Nevertheless, small-scale producers generally continue to be represented as a homogeneous class (A. Scott 1986; for exceptions to this, see Littlefield and Gates 1991 and Miles Doan 1992). Moreover, despite mention of patriarchy, family labor, and household relations, studies of small-scale production infrequently involve or incorporate analyses of power relations within the production process or of the ideology that underlies these relations. This task has been taken up to some extent by Benería and Roldán (1987), who situate the interaction of class and gender within a culturally and historically specific production system, and by Brass (1986), who proposes that kinship ideology permits and disguises the exploitation of labor in small-scale production.

Labor as Expression of Identity

In the analysis presented here, I examine the role of gender and kinship ideology in the construction of labor and power relations within a system of small-scale production in Turkey oriented toward the world market. The results of my research suggest that women's labor—paid or unpaid—is conflated with social and gender identity and with membership in social groups such as the family. In Turkey women's identity is largely expressed through complex sets of relations that involve giving and receiving labor. By exchanging labor and services, women maintain membership in social groups such as the family and neighborhood that are crucial to their economic and social survival. This association of labor with social and gender identity, in turn, provides the ideological framework for a system of cheap labor organized both in family workshops and as women's piecework.

The social group is still the primary locus of identity for the individual in Istanbul squatter districts.[4] The most basic of these groups is the family, but it can also be the neighborhood, region, or nation. A study by Duben (1982) indicates that Turkey's rapid urbanization has not weakened the emotional and economic interdependence of the traditional Turkish family. Such interdependence has increased, not just among the working class, but at all levels of society.

Despite the urban relocation of many rural families, the Turkish family also has retained its authoritarian and patriarchal character (Abadan-Unat 1986; Kiray 1976); it continues to be characterized by a sexual division of labor between two differentiated and relatively isolated spheres of activity which society clearly defines and assigns to men and women (Olson 1982).[5]

Women's social identity is primarily derived from their position within the family. This identity as daughter, mother, sister, wife is crucial for a woman to be considered a socially acceptable "good woman" (*iyi kadın*). In the squatter districts an important (although, of course, not the only) component of this crucial identity as family member is labor. A "good" woman knows how to clean, cook, serve, embroider, knit, and crochet; she bears children frequently and always keeps her hands busy. For the working-class women of Istanbul, labor, along with honor and childbearing,[6] is a central defining theme of their lives. The first things young girls in the squatter districts learn, then, are the labor skills through which they will express and maintain their personal and social identity as daughters, wives, and mothers.

Labor and the Socialization of Gender Identity

Labor is an intrinsic part of the socialization of young girls in the squatter districts and working-class neighborhoods of Istanbul. Since upon marriage a girl's labor is transferred to her husband's family, her skill and industriousness are important considerations when marriage arrangements are being negotiated. In addition to housework and caring for siblings, in the years before their marriage young girls prepare elaborate trousseaux, which involve skilled and intensive needlework, including fine stitching, crochet, and embroidery. At a very early age, many of the girls begin to contribute to family income by taking in piecework or by working on their mother's piecework. They may also work in the family atelier or in a neighborhood atelier.

When a woman marries, she has many of the same responsibilities as before, now oriented toward her husband's family rather than her natal family. Since marriage involves the negotiated redistribution of a woman's labor obligations, a married woman's relations with her natal family can be a matter of some contention between her own and her husband's kin. A woman feels that she has a moral debt to her mother to help her, yet this may interfere with her obligations to her husband's family. Both families use their status, wealth, and other relative strengths to negotiate the distance of the couple's new residence from either family and the frequency of a wife's visits to her natal family.

Once a child is born, a woman's work increases, but this is seen as an investment in the future in terms of the financial and labor contributions and emotional support one may expect from children once they become adults. The moral obligation of children toward their mother is expressed in a common verbal idiom as an unrepayable "milk debt" (*süt hakkı*[7]) for their nurturance and for the labor expended in their upbringing. The women perceive the support of sons as being crucial for their survival in old age.

Often, married women also work in their own family's atelier or take in piecework. In the atelier, their labor is unpaid, since, like women's and children's household labor, it is seen to be a natural contribution to family life. It is done within a framework of reciprocal obligation that defines and expresses membership in the family and community and that is a substantial source of support and security. The family, for example, provides young girls with money for trousseau materials, engagement and wedding celebrations, furnishings for the new home, as well as premarriage expenses and, more rarely, education.

Regular atelier employees who are not family members are paid a small wage. These minimal, even token wages are justified by pointing out that the young boys are being taught a craft in a master-apprentice relationship, which is modeled on that between father and son, while young girls are only working in order to earn money for trousseau materials.[8] In other words, their labor is evaluated by its social content within the framework of community and family.

Piecework rates also are very low, especially considering the time expended in some of the more labor-intensive activities such as knitting complex patterns. Orders and materials are brought into the community either by an intermediary who sets up a local store-front outlet or by an individual in the community whose wife distributes the materials to neighbor women. Like other relations involving labor in the family, community, and atelier, relations between pieceworkers and both outside intermediaries and neighborhood distributors are accompanied by a discourse of kinship and reciprocity.

Creating Cheap Labor

Women do not see income-producing activities such as piecework or labor in ateliers as work, in the sense of work for pay or alienated labor. They themselves insist on this distinction: In their own words, they "do" this labor (*bunu yapıyoruz*), and they "give (the product) out" (*dışarıya veriyoruz*); they do not "work" (*iş yapmak, çalışmak*).

Working outside the home among strangers makes a working-class woman morally suspect and open to ridicule. Piecework and workshop activities are recognized as labor, difficult and time-consuming, like housework. However, the women see these income-producing activities, along with the more traditional labor of house-wifery and motherhood, as being an expression of their identity as good women and of their consequent membership in a defining group as wife, mother, neighbor, and Muslim, rather than as work for which they can demand a fair financial return. As long as piece-work and atelier labor is perceived to be an expression of group identity and solidarity, rather than work, it remains morally and socially acceptable.

Since the women insist that this labor is not work, they do not keep track of the time spent or figure hourly rates for their labor. Instead, the work is taken up and put down throughout the day by different adult women and unmarried girls. It becomes integrated with the women's and girls' other activities. Wages and piece-rates therefore do not reflect the amount of labor that has gone into production. This ideology of labor—the association of relations of labor and definition of the self—is one of the factors that keeps production costs low and profits high for intermediaries, exporters, and merchants.

A Web of Mutual Support

The construction of social identity around, and its expression through, labor is one aspect of a web of mutual support that characterizes social life in the squatter districts and that ensures that individual needs are met by the group. Relations based on obligation and reciprocity bind individuals to each other as a group. They give access to labor, goods, money, useful information, partners in marriage, and other necessities.

The flow of goods, money, and services within this social web allows payment for labor (for example, for piecework, atelier labor, as well as minimum-wage employment in Turkey as a whole) to be kept below the level necessary for a family to survive.[9] People manage to cover their living expenses in part through various types of formal and informal income pooling arrangements within the family, at the workplace, and among friends and neighbors. One common form of income pooling is the "gold day," a monthly (in some cases biweekly) social event held by a group of women who are friends or kin. Each "day" is held at the home of a different member of the group in strict rotation. The hostess prepares tea, pastries, and other light foods. The women gather and spend the afternoon in each other's company, chatting, sometimes dancing to oriental music (although not all groups would find this appropriate).

Each guest brings with her a specified amount of money. This can vary from the equivalent of several dollars to quite substantial amounts, depending on the financial ability of the group; women in squatter districts will bring less to their group than middle- or upper-class women. Each woman gives the money she has brought to the hostess, who is to use it to buy gold, the traditional women's form of savings. There are also "cooking pot days," "bedsheet days," and more recently, due to the high price of gold and the reduced financial means of the population in general, a new category—"silver days."

In this way, every month one woman in the group receives a lump sum of money much larger than any she would have been able to save on her own, and which she can use to cover some large expense such as necessary household items, children's school clothes, repayment of a debt, and so on. Although ostensibly she is to use the money to buy the item specified for the "day," no one inquires whether she has actually done so. Women in more favorable economic circumstances, of course, do buy gold or other desired items for themselves or the household.

Many of the women say the money they contribute comes from their husbands, who look favorably on their participation in a savings club. Since the final disposition of the money thus "saved" generally is left to the discretion of the woman, "gold days" are also a way of rerouting money from male to female control. However, I have also heard of such "days" among groups of professional women who, presumably, contribute money they have earned themselves, and of a similar form of income pooling, without the accompanying social event, among co-workers in an office.

Families survive through pooling the income of all their members, including children. A professional couple complained that the janitor who lives in the basement of their apartment building owns a car and a VCR while they can afford neither. The janitor, his wife, and their five children all live in the two-bedroom apartment for which they pay neither rent nor utilities. All members of the family, except the very youngest children, work and pool their earnings. The wife cleans apartments and does piecework; the eldest daughter is a secretary, one son a taxi driver. The middle daughter watches the two youngest children, takes care of the household, and helps with the piecework. Even very young children, generally boys, are sometimes sent out to bring in money, hawking water, packages of tissues, chewing gum, or clotheshangers on the street, or squatting next to a scale on which passersby can weigh themselves for a small fee. Many people of all classes work at more than one job. Policemen drive cabs at night. College professors run export businesses or translate professional documents and business correspondence.

Systems of reciprocal obligation among neighbors, relatives, co-workers, and between city dwellers and their village kin redistribute the money, goods, and services needed for survival. Similarly, the traditional family system is expected to provide social security and care of the old and sick. This built-in insurance in effect makes it possible for businesses to avoid contributing to insurance, social security, or pensions.[10]

The Turkish national and political climate, an uneasy balance between secular nationalism and a conservative, religiously oriented Right, at one and the same time reinforces and discourages traditional gender expectations regarding women's work. The discourse of government programs and the media encourages women both to be "good" Muslim wives and to contribute financially to their families by working (cf. Abadan-Unat 1986:143). However, since a "good" Muslim wife does not work among strangers, this discourse about what is expected of the modern Turkish woman is clearly contradictory.[11]

These contradictory expectations lend themselves particularly well to the organization of women's and children's labor in family and neighborhood ateliers and as piecework. By means of such activities, individuals participate in the web of reciprocity and obligation and thereby express their membership in basic social groups such as the family and neighborhood, reaffirming their roles as daughters, wives, mothers, neighbors, and so on. This allows women to contribute to the financial well-being of the family, while remaining reconciled with the moral standards of the traditional family.

Home Piecework

Although no exact statistics are available, it is clear that piecework is widespread in the working-class districts of Istanbul. The first attempt to evaluate the extent of home piece-work in Turkey was undertaken by Çinar in 1989.[12] She conducted a survey of small firms hiring female homeworkers in Istanbul and estimated that there were 88,000 women pieceworkers, mostly concentrated in the export-oriented ready-made-apparel industry. This constitutes 3.10 percent of the total female population and 23.38 percent of the uneducated/illiterate female population aged eighteen to sixty-four in the city of Istanbul. However, I believe this to be an underestimation. Çinar sampled only firms registered with the Istanbul Chamber of Commerce (ICC). Many of the organized production sites in my study were not registered with the ICC, particularly those distributing piecework. Membership in the ICC was a prerequisite for obtaining export tax rebates, but most of the small neighborhood piecework distributors in my study had no direct access to export markets. Materials, orders, and finished products flowed through individual merchants and other intermediaries upward through the subcontracting pyramid to businesses of various size, organization, and legal status.

The Turkish State Institute of Statistics (SIS 1990b) in its national surveys includes categories of unpaid family workers, casual employees, and marginal-sector workers. According to the SIS, unpaid family workers, who make up 6 percent of the urban working population, are 34 percent female. Casual workers, that is, people who categorize themselves as seasonal or occasional workers, make up 8 percent of the urban work force; 13 percent of these are women. Turkish state statistics include a poorly defined category of marginal workers, based on contradictory answers to two questions.[13] Not surprisingly, given this unwieldy definition, marginal workers are seen to make up only a fraction of the urban population. Of these, however, more than half are women, most between the ages of twenty-five and twenty-nine.

However, the SIS categories are not adequately formulated to ascertain the extent of small-scale commodity production engaged in by urban women. This is true in part because of women's aforementioned reluctance to define their activities as work (the questionnaire uses the word *iş*, which the women in my study rejected as applying to their production activities), but could also be due to the fear that admitting income-producing activities to an official government representative could bring higher taxes or other negative consequences. The lack of organizational specificity of this kind of work also contributes to its valuation as leisure activity rather than as a form of labor participation. It can be expected that many of the women who described themselves as being "not in the labor force" to survey and census takers are indeed family workers or are engaged in other income-producing activities.

A more accurate reflection of the actual extent of women's small-scale commodity production in Istanbul is given by Üşümezsoy (1993). In a recent survey of a poor Istanbul neighborhood, she found that 66 percent of the women spent their free time performing some paid activity, and 64 percent of the women spent between 4 and

7 hours a day doing paid work, mostly piecework knitting. Women in Lordoğlu's (1990) study of pieceworkers in Bursa worked an average of 4.8 hours a day, with 26.3 percent working between 6 and 8 hours.

Piecework is practiced mainly by women and children and involves items that can be produced or finished by hand. By contrast, women's participation in wage labor outside the home in Istanbul squatter areas was estimated to be as low as 5.5 percent in 1976 (Şenyapılı 1981:92). In 1990 only 15.2 percent[14] of all urban Turkish women were formally employed, as opposed to 70 percent of the men (SIS 1990b).

Contemporary piecework activities in Istanbul squatter settlements have taken on forms of practice very different from older handicrafts such as those involved in trousseau preparation. I have observed the use of joint family labor in assembling, among other things, boxes of pencil leads, ballpoint pens, cardboard boxes, necklaces, and prayer beads. Women's traditional skills are utilized in stitching decoration onto shoes and clothing, knitting sweaters, and sewing clothing for export.

Many of the items produced in this way are exported to Europe, the Middle East, and the United States. This is particularly the case with knitted goods made as home piecework and clothing made with family labor in ateliers. According to a survey by the Turkish State Institute of Statistics (SIS 1990b), more than three-fourths of persons employed in Turkey and more than half of those employed in urban areas work in businesses with fewer than ten employees; and of those working in cities, 41 percent work in businesses with fewer than five employees. The survival of such small-scale producers depends to a great extent on the use of unpaid family and child labor, and especially on female family labor (Çinar, Evcimen, and Kaytaz 1988:299).

Market-oriented family production is organized in a number of different ways. At the most basic level, individual family members take orders for products from within their own personal networks, then produce the goods and distribute them. At a slightly more complex level, piecework production is organized by a neighbor, a relative, or by an outsider who opens a storefront in the neighborhood. The piecework organizer generally takes orders from and delivers the product to an intermediary who deals with the merchant or exporter.

Some piecework organizers have small ateliers for preparing the raw materials before distribution to other families. Others use family and neighborhood labor to produce goods in the atelier itself rather than as piecework, or supplement atelier production with piecework for some aspects of production.

These ateliers vary in size and number of employees, and some even have branches, for example, separate workshops headed by brothers. What these various forms of organization of labor have in common is the organization of labor according to the ideology of the traditional family, which links labor with role identity and social responsibility.

Within these ideological parameters, small-scale commodity producers survive but do not grow to any great extent. Ideological and institutional constraints ensure that this type of production remains small-scale, that labor remains cheap, and that the greatest profit is reaped by intermediaries, merchants, and exporters.

The ideological constraints involve risk-avoidance and attitudes toward income based on status appreciation rather than on profit motivation. This is often referred to in Western economic literature as *irrational* economic behavior. The institutional constraints are put in place by the government and the fully capitalist business community. They limit access to organizations, credit, and export facilities.

The Security of Mutual Indebtedness

In Turkey, piecework and family labor in small ateliers are successful because they establish and express membership in social groups, particularly the family and the neighborhood. These groups are perceived as providing reliable economic and social security within impersonal economic conditions that are seen to be hostile.

Their long-term reliability and flexibility result from the open-ended nature of such reciprocal relations. Labor and services are given not in expectation of return, but rather in expectation of indebtedness. The labor and service which characterize a mother's relationship to her son, for example, are not only gifts of love; they also create an unrepayable debt of the son to his mother (the "milk debt"). This indebtedness is the foundation of the mother's long-term social and economic security as her son grows older and is expected to support her. While this indebtedness is consciously acknowledged and pursued, it is not perceived to be a closed transaction (i.e., a gift which must be reciprocated by a countergift), but rather a natural manifestation of the roles of mother and son. Indebtedness is the currency—the common denominator—of all these exchanges. It can be saved, stored, lose value or gain it, depending on the circumstances.

I emphasize indebtedness rather than gift giving because it is precisely the practice of putting off the countergift (by which I also mean labor and other services) which joins people and groups in long-term, open-ended, elastic but durable relations. These relations create both solidarity[15] and dependence in social relationships ranging from those within the family to those in the marketplace. This constitutes a particular form of generalized exchange in which the focus is on the exchange of debts rather than on the exchange of gifts.

Evidence of this web of reciprocal, delayed obligations can be found in other areas of Turkish economic, social, and political life. Relations of obligation in society beyond the family are often represented metaphorically as family relations, as for example between the citizen and what the Turks call "Father State" (*Devlet Baba*).

In economic behavior in general, business and the extraction of profit are often expressed as open-ended personal relations through which no profit is obtained by anyone, but rather labor, money, and time are freely given. This superimposes open-ended and long-term relations of obligation on economic transactions that have an expectation of eventual payment and closure.

Conclusion

For women, labor is a major currency of social exchange by which they create solidarity and define and express their group membership, be it in the family or in the community. Although they participate in the capitalist system through their production for the local and world market, women do not gain more control over their lives through the production of income.[16] Their productive behavior is "subordinate to relations that exist independently of them" (Marx 1971:66) in the Turkish economy and the world market. But at the same time their productive behavior binds them to a communal identity and reproduces its patriarchal character (cf. Özbay 1991).

This is so because women's labor—whether paid or unpaid—is conflated with social and gender identity and with membership in social groups such as the family. Labor is a constituent part of women's membership in the social groups that provide the basis for security and identity, which are fundamental prerequisites for physical and social reproduction.

If women (and men) do not recognize a difference between wom-

en's income-producing labor and household labor, there is no obvious way for income-earning activities to substantially affect their
lives in terms of greater control over resources and decision making.
Women gain no individual control over their economic or productive lives from the work they do because their labor is in a sense the
property of the group.

The ideology of gender and kinship and its expression as a traditional family ideal in Turkey has long linked reciprocal relations
and labor obligations at different levels of society. This same ideology now ties a particular construction of social and gender identity
to world capitalism. It permits the development of a stable and flexible cheap work force requiring neither infrastructure nor material benefits and consisting of workers who pose no threat of labor
organization and make no demands as a distinct segment of the
economy. Within the ideology of the traditional family, work for the
production of surplus value is masked as labor expressing social
identity and creating social solidarity.

Small-scale production in Istanbul is embedded within a cultural
logic that provides a practical model for negotiating the contradictions inherent in the production of individual profit within a social
system based on reciprocity and mutual obligation. The actual practice of small-scale production in Istanbul brings into contradiction,
on one hand, the materialist model of capitalist enterprise, in which
labor is exploited on the basis of class, age, and gender, and on the
other hand, the social science model of reciprocity and kinship,
which emphasizes the primacy of social bonds and collective goals
over individual gain. The "model in practice" that is acted out by
the inhabitants of Istanbul squatter districts provides them with
the means to circumvent the potential for conflict and contradiction
that can arise between capitalist relations and the kinship system,
with its rules of obligation and reciprocity.

Part 2 of this book will describe the link between labor, identity,
and vectors of solidarity and competition within the primary social
group, the family. I will then discuss the implications of the practice
of reciprocity in Istanbul for social science models of exchange.
Part 3 will present certain aspects of small-scale production in Istanbul and attempt to pull together the economic and social aspects of
production in a "model in practice," using explanatory elements
from both Marxist and social-science models of economic exchange.

The practice of reciprocity, the practice of production, and the
"model in practice" by which the inhabitants of Istanbul squatter
districts circumvent potential contradictions between the requirements of kinship and capitalism reveal certain shortcomings in the

explanatory potential of present Marxist models of small-scale commodity production. These problems will be discussed in the final chapter where I suggest that the transactional system within which small-scale production occurs can be characterized by *both* market forces and collective reciprocity, with market forces ideologically articulated with and subordinated to collective reciprocity in the relations of production within the group.

Young girls at an engagement celebration.

Young boy selling socks on a busy thoroughfare.

PART 1
THE SETTING

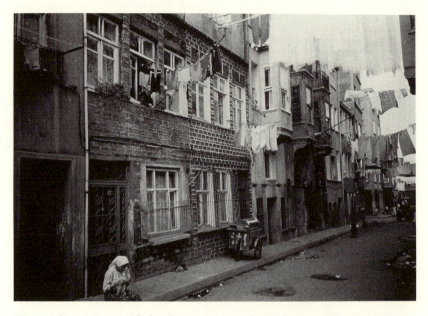

Woman knitting outside her home in a working-class neighborhood.

Distinctive dress of devout urban women.

Chapter 2
Bridge between Europe and Asia

When I approach Istanbul from the air, coasting in over the blue expanse of the Sea of Marmara, circling the great mosques of the old city as the plane banks toward the airport, I never fail to experience a sense of mystery, of descending into a mythical Orient that is a part of my personal cultural heritage. It has been bequeathed to me in the form of a Western construction of the Near East most recently given the name Orientalism. This mythical place is also called Constantinople or Byzantium. It is peopled by dark-eyed women with ropes of black hair hidden in diaphanous veils, by caliphs in robes of rich brocade.

This mythical Istanbul is a city of jewels and jewel-like colors, of passion and intrigue, the eastern terminus of the Orient Express. It is the lair of the dragon, which in the stories of my childhood guarded an enormous mound of gold, pearls, and precious stones. Seen from the Bosphorus Bridge on a cold clear winter night, the city does seem to stretch like a sinuous dragon along the side of the Bosphorus Strait, sparkling with thousands of tiny diamonds—low-voltage house lights sprinkled over the invisible hills.

The plane lands and I exit the modern airport building and hail a taxi. The taxi ride takes me into another Istanbul, also familiar, peopled with old friends as well as strangers, with people who have struggles and rewards that, while perhaps expressed differently, have fundamental similarities to the aspirations of people everywhere: material security and emotional satisfaction. This Istanbul looks different.

Leaving the airport, the taxi speeds past lines of enormous white apartment towers under construction on the flat barren land between the airport and the old city center. Each time I come to Istanbul there is more construction. (By 1986 it seemed the wall of high-rise apartment blocks reached all the way from the outlying airport to the old Byzantine walls that still demarcate the site of the old city.)

This incessant building of new dwellings still does not keep pace with housing needs, as the population of Istanbul is now growing by about a million people a year. This growth is due primarily to migration from other cities and from the economically stagnant countryside, as people are lured to the metropolis by hopes of employment.

It has been only a little more than a century since Istanbul began to grow beyond the site where, according to tradition, it was founded as Byzantium by the Greeks in the seventh century B.C. Although for sixteen centuries it was the capital of two successive empires, the Byzantine and the Ottoman, the city experienced little growth. It remained centered on a promontory separating the Golden Horn from the Sea of Marmara, an easily defensible site with a deep natural harbor, from which it controlled navigation on the Bosphorus Strait.

The Republic of Turkey was formally established in 1923, with its capital at Ankara, a city on a barren plateau in the heart of central Anatolia. The new site represented the republic's break from an imperial Ottoman past and its identification with the common people, the citizens of the new state. It was also meant to place a distance between the secular nature and Western orientation of the Turkish state and an Islamic heritage that had been focused on Istanbul. As heirs to the caliphate, the office of successor to the Prophet Muhammad, the sultans in Istanbul technically had been leaders of the Muslim faith.

Soon after the founding of the republic, the foreign embassies moved from Istanbul to Ankara, leaving behind their old mansions and villas. Although Istanbul is no longer the capital, the architectural legacy of sixteen centuries as an imperial capital is clearly visible. It is, however, being quickly submerged in the geographic and architectural consequences of the rapid population growth of the last forty years.

By the end of the last century, small areas of urbanization had appeared around the stations of the newly built railroad lines along both the European and Asian sides of the Bosphorus. This urban extension, however, was on a moderate scale, and by 1907 the city's population still did not exceed one million (Duben 1990). But within half a century of losing its position as capital to Ankara, Istanbul spread from its initial site on the promontory into an agglomeration of former villages and new settlements, small houses and enormous apartment sites stretching for miles along the coasts of the Bosphorus and the Sea of Marmara.

The inhabitants of this modern Istanbul also have a myth of their city's glorious past. Their myth is a cultural construction, as is mine. While my Western Christian culture romanticizes the Byzantine Christian Empire as well as the more exotic elements of the Ottoman Empire, Turks concentrate on the latter. Under the Ottomans, Istanbul was not only the administrative center of a far-flung empire, but the religious center for the Islamic faithful in the entire world.

Turks are proud of their history as rulers of an empire that nearly included Vienna, and Istanbul with its monuments and mosques is living proof of the greatness of their past. Schoolchildren crowd the museums and the Ottoman palaces, and historical dramas are shown on television. On Sundays families picnic in the parks surrounding the many former royal palaces, summer villas, and hunting lodges scattered along the shores of the Bosphorus.

The character of Istanbul must be understood within this accretion of the past to the present. It is a city that has been created and recreated many times, each new historical identity dramatically adding its physical embodiment to the city's features. Likewise, the city has been recreated many times as part of the discourse of the West, from its role as capital of the Roman Empire to its incarnation as Byzantium, goal of the Crusaders; from the seat of Ottoman Muslim hordes storming the gates of Europe to the symbol of a poor country sending streams of laborers to Europe and undermining European prosperity with cheap labor. The discourse of the Turkish republic also creates Istanbul in its own (often contradictory) images—as a Western city with an imperial past and as a Muslim, Ottoman city. Finally, its inhabitants are literally creating Istanbul anew each day, as more migrants arrive and more housing is built.

The city is changing both physically and conceptually, almost beyond recognition, to accommodate pressures greater than any it has faced in more than twenty-five hundred years. In the past decade in particular, the steadily increasing pace of population growth and construction threatens to overwhelm the historic character of the city, its natural environment, and its infrastructure.

The Eighth Hill: Expansion and Polarization

Until the 1950's, Istanbul—a city built, like Rome, on seven hills—was a loosely threaded necklace of separate neighborhoods and villages strung along the European and Anatolian shores of the Bosphorus. Each village or neighborhood was distinguished by a unique history and character, often reflecting its ethnic composition.

At last count (Boysan and Boysan 1987), Istanbul had swollen to encompass not seven but fifty-seven hills. Today the land appears to have been raised by the edges, tumbling millions of people and their homes so close together that there is often barely room for a sidewalk. The original neighborhoods and villages remain as points of reference for the millions of new and old residents. Every morning and evening, these people crowd the streets and broad boulevards (built in the 1950's at the start of the city's expansion) en route to homes in dozens of newly formed neighborhoods along the outskirts and in the interstices of the old.

The green wooded hills bordering the Bosphorus have become a rash of construction, official and unofficial, with luxury villas crowning the hills and poorer settlements covering the slopes. The city extends interminably to the Black Sea in the north and along the Sea of Marmara in the south, a distance of more than thirty miles; it continues to spread across the fields of Thrace in the west and the barren plains of Anatolia in the east to a total area of 887 square miles (UNFPA 1986).

Urbanization in Turkey has gained great momentum in the past thirty years. Whereas in 1950 only 18.7 percent of the population of Turkey lived in cities with a population of over 10,000, by 1980 this number had jumped to 45.4 percent. The number of cities with population over 10,000 also grew during this period from 98 in 1945 to 330 in 1980. Of the 1980 urban population, a full 63.3 percent lives in the largest cities with over 100,000 population (Keleş and Payne 1984).

The mayor of Istanbul in 1987, Bedrettin Dalan, estimated that every year 250,000–300,000 people migrated to Istanbul (*Cumhuriyet* 7/30/87).[1] The population of Istanbul was projected in 1983 to be 8 million by the end of the next decade (Keleş 1983:37), but this figure had already been surpassed by 1990.

The migrants are generally from Anatolian villages, driven to the cities by inadequate remuneration for agricultural work and by poor living conditions in the countryside, which has been long neglected under government planning and investment. In their attempts to develop and modernize Turkish society, the founders of the republic embarked on a program that emphasized industrialization and urbanization, which was seen as a means to encourage the growth of secular Western ideas and values. Later governments continued to invest in industry and to neglect agricultural development.

Rapid urbanization began in earnest after World War II with improvements in roads and communications, under the Marshall Plan, that made cities accessible to towns and villages throughout the republic. Informal networks soon developed to assist new migrants from the same region in finding housing and jobs in the city, primarily in labor-intensive low-capital businesses. Money sent back to the villages encouraged further migration. Instead of becoming centers of industrial growth as had been envisioned by the planners of the republic, Turkey's cities—particularly Istanbul and Ankara—experienced a major expansion of their labor-intensive service sectors (Keleş and Payne 1984).

Migrants to Istanbul settle in areas where rent is affordable, often after staying initially with relatives or fellow villagers (often kin) who have migrated before them (cf. Kartal 1978). In the past, this has meant that people from certain regions of the country tended to live in the same neighborhoods in the city. While this is still the case in Ankara, in Istanbul this pattern has been broken somewhat because of high rents, even in squatter areas, and a general unavailability of housing. While many migrants still have relatives living near them, kin and compatriots from the same region (*hemşeri*) are often dispersed over several neighborhoods.

The first migrants to Istanbul built houses on public land—the "eighth hill"—belonging to the State Treasury (*Hazine*). These squatter settlements were called *gecekondu*, that is, "settled at night." The appellation reflected the speed with which families and friends erected the four walls and roof by night for a fait accompli on the following day. While the Illegal Buildings Act passed in 1924 allowed the demolition of any structures built on land for which the builder did not have legal title, this law was usually interpreted in such a way that demolishing an *inhabited* building required a court order. This allowed migrants to delay and possibly frustrate the efforts of the municipality to raze their dwellings.

There is a traditional precedent for *gecekondu* settlement. Under Ottoman law these settlers would be entitled to occupy unclaimed state land to build a house or farm, as long as they paid taxes for the right to use the land (Keleş and Payne 1984). However, since such practices conflicted with the development plans and zoning regulations of modern cities, the municipality initially demolished the houses.

The enormous continuing influx of migrants, however, made this impracticable. Istanbul's first *gecekondu* areas appeared in 1946. In 1983 55 percent of the city's population was living in these areas (Keleş 1983:197). By 1987 it was estimated that one-third of Turkey's entire urban population lived in *gecekondu* housing (*Yeni Gündem* 4[73] 1987: 10).

At various times, but especially after 1983 under the Özal government, "construction pardons" were issued by the government, granting legal standing to certain houses built illegally (either without deed to the land, or without a construction permit) before that date. These pardons alternated with the bulldozer demolition of other, usually newer *gecekondu* homes.

This reflected the contradictory positions of the municipal government, which wants to discourage migration to the city, and the ruling political party and other interests, which see in the *gecekondu* areas a ready source of votes and of profit made through land speculation. At intervals, entire *gecekondu* areas are officially incorporated into the city as municipalities, despite the fact that many of the houses are built without construction permits or on public land.

In the original use of the term, *gecekondu* houses are built on public land. They are generally built of cement blocks and are plastered and painted. Often they are set inside small gardens. A *gecekondu* district resembles nothing so much as the Anatolian village its inhabitants have left behind.

The term, however, has since come to be applied to any type of housing built without a construction permit, even if the occupant has a freehold title to the land. Unauthorized *gecekondu* construction now includes multistory buildings as well and is found both in low-income and in high-income urban areas. Many luxury villas along the Bosphorus also were and are still being built without the requisite construction permits, and rumblings are heard occasionally in high places that these too should be razed, although little action has been taken.

Many neighborhoods are a mixture of houses built according to local ordinances, illegally built houses that have been given a lot deed, either through the vote-seeking generosity of a political party or through a government "pardon," and houses built without an official plan. Sometimes one floor of a house may be legally and another floor illegally built. Frequently the newspapers carry reports of some *gecekondu* areas receiving deeds for their illegally built houses while in other areas legally built homes with deeds or homes in the process of becoming legalized are accidentally razed along with illegally built homes. Thousands of families are left homeless every year in this way (cf. *Yeni Gündem* 4[73] 1987: 10–16).

For most of the landless peasants flooding Istanbul and Turkey's other major cities every year, however, building a home (usually a floor at a time) without deed to the land or without architectural permission, using family labor and materials bought piecemeal as the family budget allows, is a risk well worth taking. The *gecekondu* lottery may decree that the home be razed, but it can be rebuilt at minimal cost. At some point, a "pardon" or a political handout may lead to the migrant family becoming Istanbul property owners.[2]

The potential security resulting from freedom from high rent payments, the rental income from a second floor apartment or second *gecekondu* house, and the incorporation of a workshop or small storefront in the house, is worth the risk of being razed and having to rebuild. Some *gecekondu* areas have been razed and rebuilt as many as twelve times.

Many of these families, however, have no other housing alternatives. For a typical migrant family with four children where the mother does not work outside the home, it is not possible to pay rent as well as purchase food and other necessities on a worker's salary.[3]

The following is a typical example (taken from newspaper accounts of the incident) of the rise and fall of a *gecekondu* neighborhood and the misunderstandings and human drama involved. On the night of April 23, 1988, about fifteen hundred families who had migrated from different regions of Anatolia simultaneously built fifteen hundred houses on a large area of land belonging to the state in Yakacık, near Kartal on the extreme southern tip of Asian Istanbul. The land had been earmarked for use as a garbage dump. The people named their neighborhood "23 April." They had seen a television program on which Prime Minister Turgut Özal reportedly had said, "If a citizen builds a *gecekondu* in one night, we are obliged to give a deed" (*Cumhuriyet* 4/27/88:8). (Keleş [1983, pp. 213–214] describes a similar event that occurred in 1969.)

On April 26, the Istanbul Municipality razed all the houses to the ground with bulldozers. Police used nightsticks to scatter hundreds of angry settlers—men and women—who hurled stones at the bulldozers and blocked their paths with their bodies. One of the settlers protested saying, "[Prime Minister Özal] promised that the homes of low-income *gecekondu* possessers won't be razed. Now you come and want to raze our homes which we built with so much effort!" (*Cumhuriyet* 4/27/88:8).

Among the settlers is Halis Kara, a twenty-eight-year-old factory worker who migrated from Çankiri, about one hundred kilometers north of Ankara. Kara, who has been married ten years and has five children, explains:

I get sixty-five thousand liras minimum wage; I pay forty thousand liras rent. If there is some other solution, you tell me. . . .
Someone said that there was a very large open area here. We discussed the matter in the coffeehouses, gave the news to our

wives and friends, and all came together and divided the land. By pacing, each person took a ten-by-ten-pace parcel and marked the border with stones. In the entire area, about fifteen hundred families began to build at the same moment. Everyone took the place they saw first, or liked best, or found empty. There was no special distribution. (*Hürriyet* 4/27/88)

Like the other settlers, Halis Kara vows that if they tear the houses down a thousand times, they will rebuild them a thousand times. The authorities, in turn, say that even if the *gecekondu* houses are rebuilt, they will be torn down every time (ibid.).

The wave of migrants to Istanbul and their absorption into the urban working class has changed the character of the city. Neighborhoods were formerly characterized by ethnic or other cultural characteristics, and income was distributed fairly regularly throughout the city. This has given way to the residential polarization of the city by class and income.[4] The influx of migrants and the subsequent expansion of the urban working class has meant a lowering of the income level citywide.

Istanbul residents' gross income was twice the national average in 1978, but by 1985 it had dropped to one-fifth. In 1973 60 percent of the population of Istanbul fell into the lowest two income categories.[5] By 1987 this had risen to 84 percent. The proportion of very wealthy (in the highest income category) fell during this period from 13 to 6 percent of the population.

Over the past twenty years wealth and poverty have tended to segregate and separate out into different areas of the city. While certain parts of the city, such as the European shore of the Bosphorus north of Beşiktaş and Baghdad Boulevard on the Asian side, have always been favored by the wealthy, in 1973 these areas also still housed a sizable proportion of low- and middle-income people. By 1987, the very poor had moved almost exclusively to neighborhoods like Zeytinburnu, Beykoz, Gazi Osman Paşa, and Kartal. In 1973, 82.4 percent of the population of Zeytinburnu, one of the earliest *gecekondu* areas, was in the lowest two income categories. In 1987, 91.3 percent of Zeytinburnu was poor.

Certain neighborhoods, like Şişli and Kadıköy, became impoverished as wealthier people moved away. The proportion of wealthy (in the top two income categories) in Şişli (19.1 percent) and in Kadıköy (24.8 percent) in 1973 changed to 3.85 percent and 5.85 percent, respectively, in 1987 (*Ekonomik Panorama* 8/21/88).

As a result of migration, unrestrained construction, and the incorporation of ever new municipal areas, the ethnic and other characteristic distinctions among Istanbul neighborhoods have all but vanished, to be replaced by class distinctions. Residence in a particular neighborhood will now place a person financially, reflecting the rents current in that area.

There are exceptions to this pattern. Due to laws regulating tenant rent increases, people who have been living in the same apartment for many years still pay very low rents, even though the neighborhood may now be a luxury high-rent district. One family in Cihangir paid 125,000 TL a month rent for their spacious apartment overlooking the Bosphorus and the entrance to the Golden Horn. They had lived there for ten years. When they moved in 1986 to an apartment nearby that they owned, the vacated apartment was rented for 1.5 million TL a month, a rental rate current for apartments on that street.

In addition, because of the erosion of middle-class incomes under present economic circumstances, some young professionals, civil servants, and self-employed people such as shopkeepers and other tradesmen have been forced to rent in what they would consider undesirable neighborhoods. For this reason, except under very pressing circumstances, people will not move to another home, especially if their present rents are low as a result of long-term residence. Some middle-class cooperative housing, for example, is being built on the fringes of *gecekondu* or other poor neighborhoods. This initiates a clash between urban middle-class culture and conservative rural traditions in terms of dress, life-style, and other expectations.

To complicate the matter further, many former migrants in the older *gecekondu* areas or villages that have now been incorporated into the city proper have founded their own businesses, and some have become relatively wealthy. Because of a profound cultural difference, however, their financial success does not lead them to live in established neighborhoods of that income level. Some of these people have therefore developed a culture of their own, based on strong Islamic beliefs.

In general, it can be said that present *gecekondu* areas are inhabited almost entirely by the working class (*Ekonomik Panorama* 8/21/88). Older *gecekondu* areas or former villages now incorporated into the city tend to be more prosperous, with a higher percentage of self-employed people.[6] While newer areas retain the relatively less restrictive dress and customs of village life, older areas have become more "citified" in terms of dress and culture, exhibiting rigidly Islamic codes of dress and behavior, somewhat like the restrictive conditions found in rural towns and administrative centers.

Sites of the Study

This study was carried out in neighborhoods in different parts of the city, primarily in Ümraniye, and in Yenikent and Yolbaşı. (The latter two are pseudonyms.) I also conducted interviews of pieceworkers and atelier workers in Kadıköy, Pendik and Bağlarbaşı and did more general observation in Eyüp, Beşiktaş, and elsewhere (see map).

These areas were not chosen for their representative nature but were the neighborhoods to which I was introduced by friends and in which I therefore was given access to people's thoughts and daily lives. All are working-class neighborhoods, and in each neighborhood women were actively engaged in some form of piecework or atelier work.

Ümraniye is a large, bustling working-class neighborhood that had been a squatter area but is now fully absorbed into the municipal structure. Its population is still expanding rapidly as it absorbs new migrant families. Ümraniye's population in 1977 was more than fifty thousand, the majority of which had migrated from the Black Sea provinces and from Yugoslavia (Tümertekin and Özgüç 1977).

Indeed all of the families I came to know in Ümraniye were from the Black Sea region. This is not surprising, since I relied on one family to introduce me to others; and region of origin, as I have pointed out above, is a major social link. Most of the couples had migrated to Istanbul more than twenty years ago, after marriage. Their children were Istanbul-born. The husbands were small tradesmen, shop owners, taxi drivers, and in one case, a Koran teacher.

In these families rigid dress and behavioral codes were observed for women and girls. Their hair remained completely covered in and out of the house. Even just to sit in the garden of the house, a girl or woman would add an oversize scarf to the cotton scarf already covering her hair. She would also don a cloth coat to hide her figure. The women prayed regularly. The men tended to be pious, and one contributed heavily to the local mosque. Men and women led largely segregated lives.

Life in Yenikent and Yolbaşı was quite different. I have given these two squatter districts pseudonyms and have not marked them on the map so as to maintain the anonymity of the families I visited, since, unlike the other large and relatively impersonal neighborhoods, these are quite small communities.

Yolbaşı is a brand-new squatter settlement on the Asian side of Istanbul, on a hill overlooking a major highway. It is very poor; the women I came to know there told me that the men in the neighborhood are mostly public employees—city bus drivers or road workers. A few men and women work in nearby factories. The houses are badly and hastily constructed out of wood or cement blocks. Incongruously, there is an enormous brand-new mosque in the center of the neighborhood.

Yenikent is an older squatter district on the European side of the Bosphorus. It has existed for at least eight years, and although its lanes are still unpaved, the small hastily constructed houses are rapidly being replaced by two- and three-story apartment blocks. Everywhere are cement houses of one or two stories with antennae of thick steel cord sprouting from the roof. These will form the skeleton for pouring the retaining pillars for the next floor, when enough money has been accumulated for the materials.

The main street connecting the neighborhood to the city center is paved and lined with a few shops. A city bus services the area. Some of the houses are built without legal title to the land or without a construction permit, and the municipality occasionally razes them. There is a small but well-kept mosque on the main road.

Women in Yenikent and Yolbaşı wear mid-calf-length skirts, long-sleeved blouses, and layers of sweaters. They cover their heads with light cotton or polyester scarves that do not always entirely cover their hair. Sometimes the scarves are tied loosely or merely draped over the head.

The lanes are full of women walking to each others' homes or gathering to talk. While women and girls generally do not mingle with men outside of the family, it is not uncommon for a male neighbor to stop by the workshop (which is a public space) to chat with the husband, and for his wife and other women present to join in the conversation.

Meals are eaten together, whether or not guests are present. In Ümraniye, male guests, even if they are family members, often eat separately with the other men of the family. While the women I came to know in Yolbaşı and Yenikent were Muslims and observed religious holidays, their lives seemed in other ways to be less circumscribed by Islamic restrictions than those of the women in Ümraniye.

Like the families in Ümraniye, some of the families in Yenikent and Yolbaşı had also migrated from the Black Sea region, although more recently—between ten and fifteen years ago. These families are typical in that the Black Sea region has always been a primary source of migrants to Istanbul. Between 1960 and 1965 the majority of Istanbul's population that had been born outside of the city had migrated from the Black Sea provinces and from eastern Anatolia (Tümertekin and Özgüç 1977).

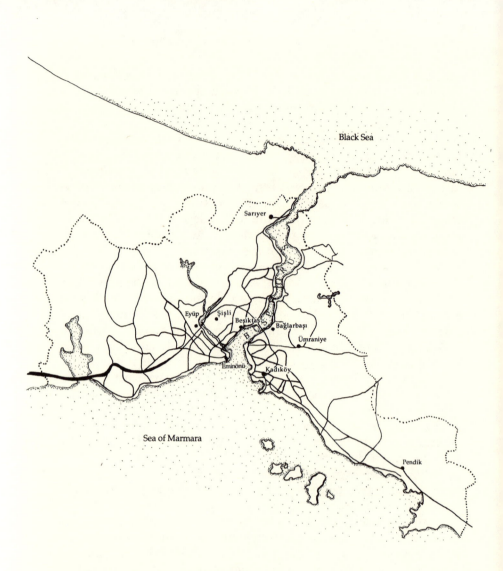

Metropolitan Istanbul. Map by Diane Watts.

PART 2
THE IDEOLOGY OF LABOR

Mothers escorting their sons to school in the morning.

Family at breakfast in a squatter home.

Chapter 3
Marriage: The House of the World

Sources of Social and Self-Identity

The nine million people who live in Istanbul orient themselves less by urban geography than by their region of origin and the presence of a particular group of people to whom they belong and from which they derive their identity. A man born, for example, in the eastern Anatolian region of Malatya remains a *Malatyalı* even though he has lived in Istanbul for twenty-five years. This links him to all other men who originated in Malatya, tying them together in a loose web of obligation for mutual aid. Social and mutual aid institutions in the form of small clubs based on region of origin can be found in most working-class neighborhoods. Men of the same place of origin gather there to smoke, drink tea, chat, and offer advice and assistance.

Women also retain regional ties through their husband's female relatives, since they generally marry either direct kin[1] or someone from their village or region. In neighborhoods with concentrations of people from a particular region, these women will tend to visit each other. Many of these women are related through complex marriage ties; through their visits, new marriages are likely to be arranged for their children, reinforcing regional cohesion within the city.[2]

The most important reference group, however, remains the family. A person is identified on documents throughout his or her life primarily by "place of birth" and "name of father." Marriage exists as the link of continuity between generations of families. Brides are "taken" (*almak*) from other families in order to bear sons that will carry on the family name and, as I will suggest here, for their labor.

Although 67 percent of all Turkish families and 73 percent of urban families are nuclear in structure (UNICEF 1991:251), the extended family remains a powerful cultural ideal (Kandiyoti 1988:

278) that has practical consequences despite separate living arrangements. Although conjugal families live in separate households, they share material support in what Abadan-Unat (1986:186) calls the "functionally extended family."

The patrilocally extended household generally has been associated with the development and reproduction of classic patriarchy.[3] However, the actual structural arrangement of family life may vary without affecting the forms of control and subordination associated with the patriarchal family system. The ideal-typical classic patriarchal family is referred to here as the traditional family, whether or not its actual structure is extended.

In the traditional family, the senior man has authority over all other family members, including younger men. A girl is given in marriage at an early age into a household headed by her husband's father (through his physical presence or de facto). She is subordinate to her husband, his kin, and especially to her mother-in-law. Women can establish their place in the patrilineage and their economic security only by bearing sons. Kandiyoti adds that "the patrilineage totally appropriates both women's labor and progeny and renders their work and contribution to production invisible" (1988:279). The hardships that younger women endure are eventually superseded by the control and authority they exert over their own daughters-in-law. The cyclical nature of power through the life cycle encourages women to internalize patriarchal values.

The valuation of restrictions such as seclusion and veiling as marks of status and honor further reinforces women's collusion in maintaining patriarchal practices. Seclusion deepens women's economic dependence on men, since it blocks access to alternative economic practices such as trading activities[4] that involve movement outside of the domestic space (Kandiyoti 1988). In Turkey seclusion generally is less strictly defined as the designation of arenas of activity appropriate to men and women. The complete seclusion of purdah is rare. "Veiling" also takes many forms, with various degrees and means of covering body, hair, and face. Within a single neighborhood it is possible to find a range of dress, from short sleeves and uncovered (*açık*, open) hair to body-enveloping coats and voluminous headscarves.

Nevertheless, there are basic shared limits in the community to the amount of "openness" that is considered proper. Beyond that limit, women can expect to be harassed by neighborhood men. In the squatter districts I visited, a sleeveless or low-cut blouse or a tight skirt would transgress the limit of what can properly be "open." These are not ironclad rules, however. Both "closed" and "open" clothing styles are constantly changing, and the boundaries of propriety are set and reset almost annually.

The traditional patriarchal family can be further qualified by intensity of religious practices. Ninety-nine percent of Turks are Muslims. Many of the Turks I know, however, do not pray regularly or go to the mosque, although they may fast during the month of Ramazan and attempt in other ways to lead a good Muslim life. Some men and women are more devout, pray regularly, and arrange for their children to attend lessons to memorize verses from the Koran. Since the members of these families place great emphasis on their Islamic character and present themselves to me primarily in that light,[5] I will refer to them here as religious families.

In these families, I have noticed that a great deal of importance is placed on upholding the moral strictures of the traditional patriarchal family described above. Women's clothing and movement outside the home, and male-female interaction are more restricted than in other working-class families in similar neighborhoods. The women interpret these restrictions as being imposed by their religion and are very concerned to live up to them. Their and other women's ability to do so is a frequent topic of conversation.

A third type of family, one not considered here further, is the conservative religious family, whose members sometimes belong to a *tarikat,* or religious sect. In these families, women may be secluded and wear a *çarşaf* (a cloak covering the entire body and exposing only the nose and eyes). Such extreme seclusion and covering is remarked upon even by members of religious families I know, often with disapproval as being too extreme and unnecessary.

This study is concerned primarily with the traditional and traditional religious family. These are ideal-typical constructions intended to express similarities in the structure of gender- and age-based relations while capturing differences in religious devoutness and in the conscious implementation of religious ideals in everyday life.

In the traditional family, parents and children retain strong emotional bonds which emphasize loyalty and self-sacrifice. A man's loyalty (*sadakat*) remains dedicated to his parents and siblings. A woman's is transferred to her husband and to her children (especially sons). The relationship between husband and wife is based more on duty (*vazife*) and obligation (*mecburiyet*) than on loyalty, especially on the part of the husband.

The basic prerequisite for the existence and continuation of the traditional family is marriage. Turkish social practices require that an individual marry, and enormous social, personal, and economic pressure is brought to bear to ensure that an individual does so. Both men and women are socialized[6] to believe that marriage is a necessary component of their identity as men and women, as adults, and as members of society. Strong public censure awaits individuals who choose to remain single (except under certain socially regulated circumstances) or to divorce.

Male and female gender identities are constructed in complementary ways. Whereas men consider themselves incapable of running a household, women see this activity as an expression of their worth as women. Men are considered incapable of taking care of themselves, thereby deemed incapable of living in a household without a woman to look after their needs. If the man is unmarried and lives alone, it is expected that his mother will provide all of his housekeeping needs such as food, laundry, cleaning, and so on, either by herself or through relatives or hired help. Thus a man, though unmarried, is never without a woman, and this relationship is expressed to a large extent through the giving and receiving of labor.

In order to have children, a man is required to marry. Since much of a wife's identity is bound up with her role as housekeeper, "a man needs a woman to take care of him" and "a man needs a wife to bear him children" are two sides of the same statement.

The idea that a man must have a woman look after his household needs is reinforced through childhood training. A boy is served by his mother and sisters, and any interest, on the boy's part, in the home and the labor involved in running a home is discouraged and even ridiculed.

There are exceptions to this, however. I was told by a number of people that there is often a division of labor in a family with more than one son. One or two of the sons will be encouraged to help with the household chores, while the other is left to take on the obviously "manly" role.

A female friend told me the following story about a man, now middle-aged, from a family with whom she was friends. It begins with an account of the praises his mother had always showered on him: "My son, how good he is, how nice. He hangs my curtains for me. Others make fun of him. He was engaged fifteen times. It didn't work." Eventually he married a woman from Thrace, and they lived in the same house with his mother. After eight years, his wife had to be treated for nervous depression. She complained of the symbiosis between her husband and his mother. Later, he received a transfer from his employer to another city, a promotion. He refused to go because he didn't want to leave his mother. The wife insisted on a separate house. Her husband answered, "What for?" The couple now live on one floor of a two-story house; his mother lives on the other floor.

While this story was being told, another woman present commented, "I've seen some other families where men are effeminate." The woman telling the story agreed. She added that this man, when young, had wanted to be a girl and had dressed in girl's clothes and had long curly hair. "I have a photograph of him dressed like that. And he always excessively praised his mother. A weird child."

What interested me in the conversation was not so much the text of the story, since it could be argued that this was indeed an unusual case (although those present assured me that it was not, at least in its general direction). I was, rather, struck by the equation of a man's doing household chores, and being in a sense "married" to his mother, with effeminacy. Thus, the examples the women gave me with the intention of showing exceptions to the statement above— that men are discouraged at an early age from taking an interest in household activities—in fact supported my conclusion that interest and assistance in the home and household are antithetical to the development and maintenance of masculinity. The man clearly was being ridiculed for being effeminate, both by others in the story and by the woman telling the story.

A man's fear of such ridicule extends into adulthood. He fears loss of his manhood (masculinity) if he engages in household labor or indeed if he spends too much time in the home. His reputation and authority suffer if people outside of the family speak of him as a *kılıbık*, or henpecked husband.

Turkish men, then, if they are to leave their natal home, must marry to do so. Most landlords will not rent to single men or women, arguing that men will not be able to take proper care of the apartment, and that single women living alone or together must be women of ill repute.

Women, of course, are able to take care of a home, having been trained to do so from an early age, but they are not considered capable of protecting themselves (against men) without the presence of a man who is bound to them by duty (i.e., either a family member or a husband). Therefore, any woman who chooses to live without this protection (*himaye*) can have no other reason than that she is engaged with men in relations that are not protective (illicit). A woman, then, in order to leave her natal home, must marry.

An unmarried man may earn a salary sufficient to allow him to rent an apartment on his own, but he is rarely able to do so. By the same token, the small percentage of unmarried women who earn sufficient money to live alone, usually find this a less attractive proposition than continuing to live with their parents. Some few women do live alone, but can do so only in certain upper-class neighborhoods and must take constant care to avoid scandal. (Only widows past childbearing age can live alone without causing comment.) Even in these neighborhoods, a woman cannot invite men into her apartment, arrive home late too often, and so on, for fear of being evicted.

One middle-class educated woman lived in an apartment which she owned in the very wealthy Bebek neighborhood, also the home of much of the foreign population. On occasion, her boyfriend came to stay with her. She took care never to allow other men into her home, so as not to invite suspicion that she worked as a prostitute. One night, she and her boyfriend had an argument and their voices reached the homes of the neighbors. The following week, the apartment administrator asked her to move out on the basis of complaints by the other occupants of the building (who had presumably been informed by her neighbors of her alleged morally reprehensible behavior). By that evening she had packed her bags and had moved out of her apartment so as not to have to face the contempt and scorn of her neighbors. Unmarried women who choose to live alone walk a tightrope of tolerance over a pit of shame.

An unmarried man living alone, on the other hand, is allowed more freedom of movement and is less under the scrutiny of his neighbors, but this means only that he walks a thicker tightrope over the pit of *others'* shame. He is considered a threat to the morals of the surrounding community because he has no legal outlet (a wife) for his presumed sexual hunger.

An unmarried middle-aged professional who lives with his widowed mother and sister has been able to save enough money to buy a home in a fashionable district in Asian Istanbul. He goes there occasionally for a few days to work and relax from the emotional pressures of his ill, housebound, and cranky mother. One day, his sister went to the house to water the plants. As she was unlocking the door, the neighbor woman came out and asked her who she was. Upon being told that this was the homeowner's sister, the woman began to shout at her, "Do you think I believe that?! Honorable families live in this neighborhood. How dare you come here!" The sister, shaken, reported this to her brother who, shaking his head in frustration, sighed, "You can't live anywhere in peace." Later, he knocked on the neighbor's door and confirmed that the woman she had seen was indeed his sister.

In cases like this, the woman is blamed as the instrument of dishonor, since summoning her is considered only natural for an unmarried (and therefore sexually unsatisfied) man. It is likely also that the man's mother is blamed, since she has not succeeded in finding her son a suitable bride.

Marriage, then, is seen as both a biologically necessary state and an obligation to one's family and to society. Except in the very small elite Westernized social group, marriages widely continue to be arranged, although generally with the concurrence of the prospective bride and groom.[7] These days in the urban centers, prospective brides and grooms usually are allowed to meet once in the presence of both families and are given the opportunity to accept or refuse marriage.[8] This meeting is not held in the girl's home but at the home of a close relative so as to preclude gossip that the girl had rejected many suitors, leading to a reputation of capriciousness.

Marriage generally occurs at an early age (in order to anticipate the temptations of the flesh and to prevent dishonor). Until recently, over 50 percent of Turkish women married between the ages of fifteen and seventeen (Abadan-Unat 1986:173). More recent statistics (1988) show that the mean age of marriage for women has risen to eighteen (Hacettepe 1989:29–30). Men marry at about age twenty-two (UNICEF 1991:253), after completing their military service.

The lack of much previous personal connection with a spouse lends itself to a marriage relationship based on duty and obligation, rather than on sharing and communication (these are also precluded by the structure of daily life, the division of labor, etc.). The relationship between husband and wife is expressed as a culturally imposed and rewarded division of labor and responsibility.

Failure of either side to live up to their nuptial role, for example, as breadwinner or bearer of children, can be made grounds for divorce.[9] However, because of the social stigma and financial and legal disadvantages of divorce, women often choose to remain married even though the marriage has deteriorated completely—even in cases where the husband is chronically unemployed, alcoholic, or violent, openly lives with a mistress, or has run away. A man may remain married, but maintain a mistress or take a second wife (by religious rites; polygamy is illegal in Turkey[10]).

While there is great social pressure to marry and to remain married, marriage also is an alluring prospect for a girl from a traditional family. A girl attains adult status through marriage. She is transformed from a child (*kız*, female child, also means virgin) to an adult through the alchemy of being touched by, being looked at directly, and coming under the "control" and "care" (both can be translated using the same term, *sahip olunmak*) as well as "protection" (*himaye*) of a man.

A married woman is a respectable woman, a person whose opinions carry weight among other similar women. Marriage gives her a certain status, although in a controlled and restricted way, in the eyes of her world. A woman who is no longer a child but who is not married is not respected in the same way, nor is she listened to. An unmarried forty-year-old woman who is a professor at a major university lamented that "at family gatherings no one listens to my opinion, even if it's a subject that I have some expertise in. Instead, they listen to my cousin's wife who didn't even finish high school. Just because she's married and I'm not." Delaney (1987:42) writes that in Turkey "unmarried women are socially invisible."

A married woman has her own home[11] where she can receive guests (relatives or neighbor women). "To serve" (*hizmet etmek*) in one's own home is inextricably bound up with status; "to be served" is an honor. Women serve their husbands, their children, and their guests.

The most important benefit of marriage (for both men and women) is children. The birth of a child marks continuity of his family to the father, and the beginning of her family to the mother. Children represent many things, from the conferring of true adulthood on their parents, and community respect and status, to economic continuity and security and a later sharing of labor.

When a man and woman marry, they are said to enter the *Dünya Evi. Dünya* translates as "people," "this life," and "world, earth"; *ev* is house. Marriage, then, is entering "the house of the world"—the house of life and people. Unmarried men and women remain in the class of children, on the bleachers of life, still learning or incapable of joining the game.

Apportionment of Labor

After marriage, a woman's ties with her natal family generally are expected to become attenuated, and her duties and obligations are transferred from her natal home to her husband's household and to his parents and other kin. However, even though a married woman owes her complete attention and labor to her husband, children, and mother-in-law, the mother-daughter relationship remains important even after marriage. This results in competing demands for a woman's time and labor, which the woman (and her natal family) must negotiate carefully in order to avoid friction with her husband and his mother.

A woman has many of the same responsibilities and duties and a man many of the same privileges as before marriage. Men are served by their wives instead of (or in addition to) their mothers and sisters. Women serve their husbands, his relatives (particularly his mother), male children, their own guests, and those of the husband's family, just as before marriage they served their parents, younger or male siblings, and their parents' guests.

A married woman's range of movement outside the home remains constricted, just as it was restricted by her father and brothers after age nine or ten outside her natal home. She may, however, enter a cycle of visiting close neighbors and relatives that provides much movement outside the home, if not far afield.

Despite the advantage of marriage for a girl to become a social adult with her own home, the disadvantages of marriage are legion, especially before the birth of a male child, the means by which a woman can better her situation in the patriarchal family.

At marriage a woman's relations with her natal family are often curtailed. This differs from Arab culture, which is characterized by much greater mutuality among affines. Among the Arabs, a woman's natal family retains ties with their married daughter as well as an interest in protecting her honor (Meeker 1976). A Turkish woman's position at marriage resembles the status of the "stranger bride" typical of prerevolutionary China more than it resembles that of the Arab woman who through endogamy retains ties with her natal kin that may strengthen her position in the patriarchal household (Kandiyoti 1988). Meeker and Kandiyoti relate this difference to a lower rate of endogamy among the Turks than the Arabs.

If a Turkish woman is a migrant to the city, communication with her natal family may be cut drastically. One woman who migrated to Istanbul at marriage when she was sixteen has lived in this or another *gecekondu* district for twenty years. In that time, her mother has visited her only once, the previous year, for two weeks. Every year in the summer, the woman travels to the Black Sea coast to help her husband's family harvest and process their sugar beet crop. She stays for three months. In that time, she is able to visit her natal village, a seven-hour trip by bus, only once for one week.

But even if a woman's natal family lives nearby, her husband may forbid her to see them. Failure to obey may result in a severe beating or, according to newspaper reports, even death. Some husbands, however, do permit their wives to visit their natal families. I will suggest in the following chapters that a wife's relationship with her natal family and the reaction of her husband reflect less an arbitrary administration of male prerogative or the relative prevalence of endogamous marriage than a struggle over the apportionment of a woman's labor.[12] An important factor in this struggle is the social and financial strength the woman's family can bring to bear to retain access to their daughter's labor, assistance, and moral support.

When a woman goes as a bride (*gelin*,[13] literally "the one who came") to her husband's home, she becomes responsible for meeting her mother-in-law's demands for labor and service. This is the case whether or not they live under the same roof. The relationship between marriage and a woman's labor is expressed in the following saying:

> Delikli taş yerde, gelinlik kız evde kalmaz. (Just as a stone with a hole [grinding stone] can't stay on the ground, a girl of marriageable age can't stay home.)

This was explained to mean that, like a grinding stone which is always in use grinding bulgur (cracked wheat), a woman of marriageable age inevitably becomes a *gelin*. The connection between the labor function of a grinding stone and that of a *gelin* is clear.

Whenever possible, the *gelin* is situated close to her in-laws and far from her own parents. This is meant to resolve any possible contradiction in labor demands. A woman's sense of obligation toward her natal family, however, and particularly toward her mother, is very strong. After marriage, a woman will try to maintain as much contact with her natal family as possible. At the same time, her parents will attempt to negotiate at the time of the wedding to have her as near to them as possible. This is particularly the case when the girl's labor is needed in the natal household. Where the bride's family has clout or the groom's family is weak or distant, the daughter often is able to remain close by, usually in the same neighborhood.[14]

The following three examples will illustrate the negotiation of contradictions that emerge from the redistribution of a woman's labor at marriage. The first two examples show how it is possible for a girl's parents to negotiate her proximity after marriage. The norm—an attenuation of ties between a married woman and her natal kin—is illustrated by the third example.

In the first example, a family that needed to retain the labor of their eldest daughter, Güler, arranged for her to marry a distant relative. The young man was in a financially inferior position, and his family was not only geographically distant but also without a strong family head to intercede for him. This situation allowed the parents of the bride to arrange for their daughter to remain in the same neighborhood and continue to work for her natal family.

In the working-class section of Kadıköy, Deniz works as a concierge in a small apartment building. She receives a token salary, but rent and utilities are free. Her husband is a clerk for a small business in downtown Eminönü. They have four children, three girls and one boy, the youngest. Deniz supplements her salary by cleaning and doing laundry for the building tenants and earns a small salary for taking care of an old woman in a nearby neighborhood. She also cleverly manages the money sent by the absentee landlord for repairs and other purchases so that she is able to keep some of it. All of these sources of income combined enable the family to survive and to save for their children's wedding expenses.

The two oldest daughters help her clean the apartments, and often the elder daughter, Güler, sixteen, takes on all the building chores as well as the cleaning and laundry while her mother is away taking care of the old woman.

Güler was married last year to a distant relative, a young man whose father had died and whose mother lived in a village far to the east. The man's elder brother, now head of the family, did not interest himself in his younger brother and had provided very little financially for the wedding.[15] Güler's family, then, bore the brunt of the expenses for the wedding preparations.

Although Güler had confided in me months before that she wanted to live up the Bosphorus in a home of her own, the young couple rented an inexpensive ground-floor apartment in the house of Deniz's relative in the same neighborhood, a five-minute walk away. When I asked Güler why they hadn't moved up the Bosphorus as she had wanted, she answered that it was better this way; she would miss her family otherwise.

Before long, I noticed that Güler was present in the building as though she had never married and moved away. She spent all day in her parents' apartment, cleaning, washing dishes, taking care of her younger siblings. She also continued to clean the other apartments and to do their laundry. The money for these services continued to be paid to her mother. When I asked her why she didn't spend more time in her own new home, she said she missed being with her family. After a pause, she added, "I do get tired. After I leave here, I go home and clean and cook there." But then a smile lit up her face again and she said, "But I'm glad I can be so close to my family."

In a more fashionable middle-class neighborhood, Banu, a twenty-seven-year-old university graduate, was evaluating a marriage proposal from a man whom she barely knew but whose family was quite wealthy, in the construction business in the eastern city of Erzurum. Banu was hesitant because the man was from the conservative east and she was afraid the marriage would be restrictive.

Banu thought of herself as a modern Westernized woman. How-ever, despite her modern dress, education, and ambitions (for ex-ample, to go to England to learn English), she lived daily under severe restriction of movement imposed by her unmarried conser-vative elder brother and her diabetic widowed mother.

Her mother never left the house and demanded constant care and attention, her continual complaints interspersed with sharp, angry commands. Banu felt guilty leaving the house even for a few hours. The apartment was always dark, the curtains drawn, with a white sheet laid out for the mother on the couch in front of the tele-vision set in the living room. The apartment smelled musty and of medicine.

This was the choice with which Banu grappled: her mother's home with its restrictions predicated on honor (*namus*) and guilt, or marriage with an unknown man who she worried might also restrict her (although she said he had agreed to allow her to work,[16] go to school, and see her friends, maybe even go abroad to learn English).

In the end, she accepted the proposal because, as she pointed out matter-of-factly, even if the marriage is also restrictive, at least she will have her own home. Later she said, "Well, you know, he's a person of a certain status in society." She turned dreamy-eyed and murmured, "It would be really nice to have something like that re-flected on one as well."

As the wedding preparations proceeded, I ventured to Banu's brother that perhaps Banu should have waited and gotten to know the groom better first before making up her mind. He muttered something long and involved, the gist of which was that one should investigate people before one makes a decision, not after. (It had emerged at the engagement party that the groom's two maternal un-cles had polygamous marriages.) Knowing the brother, however, I also suspected sour grapes at being left to deal with his mother alone. I asked if the young couple had found an apartment yet. "Yes," he said, brightening, "she'll be living in the same neighbor-hood. We found an apartment right on this street." After a pause, he added protectively, "We want her near here, with us."

In both the cases above, the women's natal families were able to negotiate their daughters' proximity and continued access to their labor, partly because of the geographic distance of the grooms' kin. In the following example, a woman's ties with her mother are greatly attenuated even though she lives only blocks away. Aynur and Ali are a professional couple in their forties who still engage in a basic debate, eighteen years after their marriage, about labor given by Aynur to her mother, who lives nearby, and which is begrudged by Ali, and labor demanded by his mother, who lives farther away but comes to stay for long periods, and which is resented by Aynur. They have three children.

Aynur comes from a well-to-do upper-middle-class family, and her husband from a poorer family. Aynur's mother wanted her to marry in her own class, even though the prospective groom was a young professional like her daughter. This attitude still sticks in her husband's throat whenever the family benefits from Aynur's widowed mother's relative wealth, whether through gifts, loans of money, a car, or a summer house.

Although Aynur's mother lives only three streets away, her husband resents her going to see her, so she visits only rarely. The mother only visits her daughter's household on holidays. She has no other children. She baby-sits her daughter's youngest child, however, every day while the parents work. The brief moments picking up and dropping off the child are all the time Aynur has to spend with her mother.

Ali's mother, on the other hand, although she lives farther away, places periodic heavy demands for services on her son's family. She has two other children, a son and a daughter, whom she also visits. She phones to ask her son to run errands for her, for example to drive over and pick up her shoes to be repaired. Every few months she calls to announce that she is coming to visit and then stays for up to a month. When she arrives, she becomes "ill" and is unable to do anything around the house, often requiring her meals at different times and served in her room. Both her son and his wife believe that this is not a true illness because they have taken her to several doctors, who found nothing wrong. At the end of her stay she invariably becomes "well," taking up her rounds of visiting friends all over the city. The son does not get along well with his mother and resents her intrusions because they cause tensions between him and his wife, but he feels he cannot criticize her behavior to her face or ask her to leave.

Aynur has a full-time job. She also does all the housework, cooking, washing up, laundry, ironing, and patching, in addition to taking care of the three children. Her mother-in-law demands service and does not lift a finger to help.[17] It seems to both husband and wife that she even attempts to sabotage Aynur's work. For example, when the mother-in-law is asked to watch the youngest child for the day, while she is staying in their home, she invariably chooses the moment that Aynur is leaving for work to begin her prayers. Aynur must wait until she is finished praying and can take charge of the child. This makes Aynur late for work.

The couple also resents Ali's mother's capricious financial demands, such as a very expensive new pair of glasses although her prescription had not changed. Once her mother-in-law told Aynur to her face that she came to stay with them because, "I will eat up my son's money. Why else did I bear a son?"

These three examples illustrate the contradictions that emerge from the redistribution of a woman's labor at marriage and the strategies families use to retain a woman's proximity and access to her labor. The inherent conflict between her mother's moral claim and her mother-in-law's customary claim to her labor is negotiated by adjustments and strategies of time and space. These strategies also reflect the relative advantages of class, wealth, status, and strength of the families involved.

In the case of Güler, her marriage to a man without means, whose family was physically distant and disinterested, allowed Güler's family to continue to use her labor. Since Banu's in-laws lived in a faraway city, her family was able to dictate that initially she live near them in order to take care of her housebound mother. Wealthy parents usually try to keep their children nearby by building an apartment building or large house with an apartment set aside for each son and his *gelin*.[18] Thus if Banu's in-laws had lived in Istanbul, she might well have been separated from her natal family and bound spatially to her in-laws.

Although Aynur's mother lives near her, the major claim to Aynur's labor (beyond that of her nuclear family) comes from her mother-in-law. Although her mother-in-law lives farther away, she neutralizes this distance by taking advantage of the fact that her son and his wife have a car, and by living with them for long periods of time. The husband's enduring resentment of Aynur's mother's class-consciousness leads him to punish her by withdrawing her daughter's contribution of time and labor. Nevertheless, he accepts Aynur's mother's labor (baby-sitting) and financial help.

The transference of duty and service from the *gelin*'s mother to her mother-in-law, then, is a process fraught with emotion and conflict, and generally leads either to simmering resentment or to a subtle strategy of pressure and resistance. Of all the married women I spoke to, not one praised her mother-in-law. Some spoke bitterly about their mothers-in-law or explained that they were not able to interfere because they lived too far away. Men, too, have complaints about their mothers-in-law, predicated upon alleged interference in family affairs.

The conflict between the bride and her husband's family is particularly intense in Turkey, as it was in prerevolutionary China (cf. Diamond 1975), because of the relative isolation of the bride from her own kin.[19] The bride enters her husband's household as a basically dispossessed individual whose labor is appropriated by the patrilineage to the greatest extent possible.

The reason for the resentments and battles which arise are to be found in the contradictory claims to a woman's labor. A mother has a moral and emotional claim to her married daughter's labor, especially if she has no grown sons, but this claim may not be accepted or acknowledged by the daughter's husband and his mother. When I asked a middle-aged man raised in a traditional middle-class family what a mother expects from her married daughter, he answered as follows: "She expects her daughter's husband to protect her daughter and not to treat her badly." I repeated the question, emphasizing "daughter." He answered, "Nothing."

This answer reflects the social construction of a bride's position vis-à-vis her natal household; there are no further expectations from the daughter. Nevertheless, women develop a particular closeness with their daughters, since they are always together and provide assistance and companionship for each other. This bond of affection and caring leads to the expectation of assistance from daughters and a sense of obligation of daughters to their mothers.

When I asked what a mother expects from a married son, the same man answered, "She expects her daughter-in-law to show respect to her son and herself. She expects her son to dedicate a certain amount of time to her." I asked how much time. "It depends on the people."

It is clear also from the form of the answers, at a tangent to the questions, that what a mother expects from a married child, at least according to the man's point of view, is a *condition*, rather than particular behavior. In this condition of married life, husband and wife have certain duties to fulfill; the man is to provide security and spend time with his mother. The *gelin* is to have no ties with her own mother and to show respect to her husband and mother-in-law. As we shall see below, however, a woman's view of her relationship with her mother after marriage may differ greatly from this.

Aytan is a married university-educated woman who has not left her working-class environment. She told me that her widowed mother, who lives a fifteen-minute bus ride away, expects her to come for spring and fall cleaning, and to help with the yearly spring painting of the walls of her mother's home, grimy from a winter's heating with a coal stove.

She also helps her mother clean the house, prepare food or cakes, and make tea before religious holidays and for a *mevlud*, a religious memorial service usually held in the home and attended by a large number of women. A daughter also helps her mother when she is ill. Aytan: "These are a daughter's *emeği* to her mother." (*Emek* is translated as "work, labor, trouble, pains," but is used here to mean a contribution of labor as homage to a person who has a right to this labor.) "What kind of daughter is it that doesn't help her mother?"

A daughter does not have the same sense of obligation to her father. Aytan: "If you show respect to your father, that's enough. That's all. If he's ill, you say *Geçmiş olsun* [May it pass]."

Aytan's three sisters live in Germany or in another part of Istanbul. She has no brothers. Her mother once complained to me that none of her sons-in-law or other daughters ever help her and that she relies completely on Aytan. She launched into a long litany of praise for her daughter. Aytan confided in me that her mother once had even told her never to have children and that she is sure this is because "when daughters have children this draws time and attention away from their mothers." The mother-daughter relationship remains important even after marriage. It is expressed in the form of labor and is felt as a moral responsibility: "She needs me."

A man's mother, however, has a customary, that is a socially constructed, claim to a *gelin*'s labor, especially if they live in the same household. The *gelin*'s responsibilities toward her husband and his family are clearly delineated and predicated equally clearly upon labor and service. A *gelin* is expected to be obedient, respectful, silent, and modest. The following saying was reported as being used by women to complain about their daughters-in-law:

Bizim gelin
Bizden kaçar
Başını örter
Kıçını açar

(Our bride
Runs away from us
She covers her head
And exposes her behind)

This refers to what is perceived by the mother-in-law to be inconsistent behavior of the *gelin* with regard to respect and modesty; for example, if the *gelin* leaves the room (a sign of respect) and covers her hair (modest behavior) but doesn't wear stockings, exposing her bare legs.

The *gelin* is expected to keep her own home and often the home of her husband's parents and sometimes those of his siblings spotlessly clean and to help them with cooking and other chores. Aytan: "My older sister's landlord's daughter is seventeen. She's newly married. The mother-in-law lives on the top floor of the same apartment building, but I haven't seen the girl in her own home yet. Whenever I go, she's at the mother-in-law's. Either she's ironing or doing the laundry, or washing the dishes, or lighting the stove. And when I went one day, the mother-in-law's own daughter [literally "the home's own girl"] was there. That girl was sitting down. The *gelin* was ironing. And doing *all* the ironing!"

The *gelin* must have food ready to be served at any time if her in-laws come by. Ideally, she should serve this food quietly and withdraw. In a traditional religious household, if a second man joins the husband—even if that man is his father or brother—the men eat alone and the women wait in another room so as not to be seen by them. In less devout families, the same effect is achieved by the women's continual presence in the kitchen preparing to serve the various courses that make up a typical Turkish meal. In some families, the *gelinler* serve the meal and then eat separately or in the space of time between serving the last dish and clearing the table.

A *gelin* is also expected to keep her hands productively busy with such activities as knitting and crocheting, in addition to cooking and cleaning. There is a saying used by neighbors but especially by a mother-in-law when angry, to imply that a woman is unable to use her hands productively:

El eli üstünde, el amı üstünde oturuyor.
(She sits with her hand upon her hand and with her hand upon her cunt.)

Aytan: "To be a good woman [*iyi kadın*] you have to have a skill [*maharet*]. It's simply an inseparable necessity for a woman." To sit with one's hand resting upon the other in one's lap is a proper attitude of respect. The saying turns this around, implying at one and the same time that the woman is actually being disrespectful by touching herself immodestly and that since she does not possess the characteristics (*maharet*) of a good woman, what remains is only her physical attribute of being a female, with its implication of a woman stripped of social roles, a loose woman.

In the classic patriarchal system where women collude in and reproduce their own subordination (Kandiyoti 1988), means of active resistance are blocked either physically (for example, through spatial restrictions) or normatively (through the requirements of honor). Kandiyoti writes that, like women in prerevolutionary

China, Turkish women rely on interpersonal strategies to manipulate the affection of their husbands and sons in order to maximize their security. Kandiyoti refers to this as the women's half of the patriarchal bargain: protection in return for submissiveness and propriety.

A large part of patriarchal expectation is acted out, however, between the bride and her mother-in-law. Since the patriarchal bargain also revolves around expectations of labor, this provides another arena for a woman's passive resistance to the demands of patriarchy.

Aytan suggested that showing disrespect by sitting "hand over hand" demurely all day is one way a *gelin* gets back at her mother-in-law. She is overly demure and respectful—and does no work, fulfilling one expectation to such an extent that the other (and from the mother-in-law's perspective functionally more important) expectation falls by the wayside. This might lead the mother-in-law to complain simply, "El eli üstünde oturuyor" (she sits with her hand upon her hand).

Resistance can also take the opposite form. A mother-in-law in a working-class neighborhood complained about her *gelin:* "She knits like crazy. She's lost her senses and knits day and night. Her eyes don't see anything else. She knits like crazy morning and evening. She's crazy about the money." (The *gelin* was knitting on a piecework basis.) Again, resistance takes the form of an extreme expression of a desirable trait: a *gelin* is expected to be industrious and not sit *eli boş* (empty-handed).

The Labor Value of Children

Once a child is born, a woman's labor and responsibility increase, but this is seen as an investment in the future *maddi* and *manevi* support—that is, financial and labor contributions and moral support expected from one's children when they become adults.

A female attendant at a small *hamam* (public bath) in a working-class neighborhood on the Asian side once advised me as she scraped my skin with a *kese* (a rough washcloth), "Never get married." She repeated it for emphasis. I asked her the obvious question: Was she married? Yes, she said. She indicated that she didn't like her husband. I asked her why she got married. She said that she had a stepfather, and "You know . . ." She made a broad gesture of helpless condemnation. (Mistreatment and sexual molestation of stepdaughters by stepfathers is a commonly expressed fear, and I understood her to be indicating a problem of that sort.) "They mix into everything." She married at fourteen to get away, and had her first child at fifteen. She now has four children. The oldest is twenty-one. That made her thirty-six, only two years older than I was, but she looked much older—in her forties. Her body was overweight and shapeless. Her breasts drooped. Her face looked kind when she smiled and had traces of what could have been a merry personality, but mostly her face was resigned and weary. Her two oldest girls are married, she continued. She has a son aged eighteen and a girl of fourteen. I asked her (having misunderstood something she said) if she was planning to marry the girl off so young. "No," she exclaimed, "I won't give the girl in marriage. I need her to be at home while I work here."

The expectations a woman has of lifelong financial and labor assistance and emotional loyalty from her children often lead to struggles over these between a woman and her children's spouses, particularly daughters-in-law. One arena of struggle is in the control of space and time. In many traditional families, a *gelin* often sees her husband only at night. He remains away from home in the evenings, wandering the streets or meeting his friends. After 9 P.M., the streets of Istanbul become the sole province of thousands of men wandering about, standing in small knots, talking, sitting in coffeehouses behind steamy windows or in restaurants that serve *rakı*, the national anise-flavored alcoholic beverage. In religious traditional families, however, such behavior is not generally tolerated, and the husband is expected to eat and spend the evening with his family.[20]

A mother often encourages this pattern of spatial and temporal separation of her son and his wife in order to prevent the development of emotional intimacy between them. A mother hopes thereby to remain the sole focus of her son's loyalty, securing her future material security and moral support. If mother, son, and *gelin* live in the same home, this struggle of space and time is intensified.

In addition to the struggle over control of space, time, and labor, married women face other difficulties. Physical violence against women is prevalent in Turkish society, both for young girls at home and in marriage (cf. Yüksel 1991). Physical violence within marriage is not only widespread, but is socially accepted as a husband's right (implying that the woman is at fault). Two popular sayings support the right of men to beat women in their family:

Kızını dövmeyen dizini döver.
(He who doesn't beat his daughter will be sorry later.)

Kadının sırtından sopayı karnından sıpayı eksik etmiyeceksin.
(You mustn't let a woman be without a child in her womb and
a stick on her back.)

Upper- and middle-class educated women began in 1987 to cam-
paign in the streets against the beating of women; but while their
protest marches were given wide news coverage, most people I spoke
to think it had little effect on actual practice. The group that organized the marches, Women in Solidarity against Beating, published
a book, *Bağir! Herkes Duysun!* (Scream! Let Everyone Hear You!), in
1988. The book contains interviews with women who have been
beaten by husbands, fathers, brothers, and even by mothers- and sis-
ters-in-law. The women relate the circumstances surrounding the
beatings and the attitudes of those around them.

One of the reasons many women mentioned for being beaten is
the mother-in-law's exclusive relationship with her son. Wife-
beating is sometimes condoned if not praised and encouraged by the
husband's mother, who has a vested interest in claiming her son's
primary allegiance and in keeping the conjugal bond secondary.

Generally, the fault for violence is seen to rest with the woman.
In November 1988 an upper-class woman, nine months pregnant,
was driving to the Istanbul airport to pick up her husband. According to eyewitness accounts reported in the newspapers, a truck
driver harassed her (a common activity of male drivers in a country
where women drivers are still rare) and eventually pushed her off
the road, leading to her death and that of the fetus.

The newspapers, however, unanimously treated the incident as
being the fault of the woman for driving while she was pregnant and
published medical opinions, along with photographs of the male
doctors interviewed, about the dangers of high blood pressure, potential fainting spells, and so on that indicate that pregnant women
should not drive.

Although the eyewitness reports are briefly mentioned and clearly
indicate intent to intimidate, neither the newspapers nor the police,
judging from their statements to the press, were interested in pur-
suing the truck driver. This lack of interest was so glaring, however,
that a few days later columnists in two major newspapers remarked
upon the skewed reporting. Nevertheless, nothing further was heard
about the case, and it is possible that the truck driver was neither
sought nor found. In the public's mind, the woman, not he, was
guilty.

Beatings within the family are perceived by both men and women
to be legitimate (*meşru*) and right (*haklı*). As one thirty-year-old

married woman who had been beaten by her brother-in-law, uncle, and cousin put it in her interview for the book (*Bağır!* . . . 1988): "It's traditional and customary. A woman who isn't beaten, isn't a woman. That's what our elders say."

With the scale of marriage weighted so heavily on the side of duty, labor, emotional distance, and physical violence, why then, apart from the social pressures mentioned above, do women marry? Indeed, why is there a chorus of voices urging the unmarried researcher to marry as soon as possible, equal to the chorus of voices urging her *never* to marry (a moderate course is never suggested), and sometimes issuing from the same throats? Most girls want to marry in order to establish a social identity as adults and to have their own home. But the most important reason for marriage is to have children, particularly sons. This establishes the women as mothers, a respected social identity, and gives them a source of companionship and security. A son also gives a woman status and leverage within her husband's family and household.

One of the most vocal and impassioned of the voices urging marriage is that of Füsün. She is married to a devout man who has worked himself up from employee to part owner of a small but prospering plumbing supplies store. Füsün is thirty-nine and has two sons. She was born in a village on the Black Sea not far from Istanbul and moved at her marriage to the working-class neighborhood where she still lives.

Although the family is relatively well off and has just built a small home, it is furnished simply and cheaply like all the other working-class homes in the area. Regardless of the weather, Füsün wears inexpensive long, patterned skirts, layers of sweaters, thick stockings, and sensible shoes. She wears a headscarf at all times, even in her home. Among close family (although not her in-laws) and female friends, she wears only a light white cotton head covering but adds a larger opaque polyester scarf when someone else arrives or if she goes out of doors. Her husband buys all of her clothing, and although she has wanted a black or dark blue sweater for some time, her husband refuses to buy it because he doesn't like those colors. Füsün has no money of her own beyond what her husband gives her for the household.

In many respects, her husband can be considered a good family man. He is a quiet man who spends almost all his spare time with his wife and sons. He is known for his kindness toward his wife (who is often ill) and toward her friends and people in general. He donates a great deal of money to the local mosque and Koran courses.

The household is run in very traditional fashion, with men and women generally either in separate rooms (if strangers are present) or engaged in separate activities. Füsün can leave the house during the day to visit nearby friends and neighbors. She frequently attends religious services at other women's homes and goes to engagements and weddings with her husband and sons (who disappear into the separate men's hall some distance away and only reappear when it is time to leave). However, Füsün also spends a great deal of time at home because of her illness. Her house is often full of visitors, usually including her sister, who lives nearby, and her daughters. Sometimes, her mother comes to visit from the village.

One day, at her niece's engagement party, Füsün and I were standing behind a raised railing in the front of the room, watching a few young girls dance (raised wrists and a tentative, unprovocative movement of the hips). The room was crowded with hundreds of women from the neighborhood and those bused in from the village, a sea of black coats and large white cotton headscarves (the dress of their region of origin). Only the future bride and the young girls dancing stood out, the bride in a sequined violet dress and the other girls in simple skirts and blouses, with patterned synthetic headscarves.

Füsün, leaning on the railing and watching the girls, said sadly to no one in particular, "These young girls dance and laugh. They do all kinds of things! But when you get married, the pleasure of it is gone. A person extinguishes." I looked at her in surprise and asked her why she then told people they should get married, reminding her that she was always pressuring me to do so. Füsün looked at me without turning her head and stated simply, "How else can you establish a nest [*yuvayı kurmak*]?"

Chapter 4
The Patriarch

In many ways, the ultimate purpose of marriage for both men and women in Turkey is to produce a son that will extend the patrilineage. Delaney, in her (1987) study of attitudes toward procreation in Turkey, writes that children are perceived to come from the seed (semen) that is planted in a woman's fertile "soil."

> Women are imagined as vessels through which life is made manifest. The life incorporated in seed is theoretically eternal, provided men produce sons to carry it down the generations. "A boy is the flame of the line, a girl the embers of a house." Seed is a kind of living torch that is passed from father to son *ad infinitum*. *Sülale*, the Turkish word for patriline is, according to Rahman, derived from the Arabic and means reproductive semen. Rather than the spark that perpetuates the line, women are the fuel consumed in the process. If a man has no sons, it is said *ocağı sönmüş*—his hearth has extinguished. It is a fate worse than death. (Delaney 1987:39)

"Establishing a nest" is therefore also important for men, for this is the only way in which they can pass on the essential "spark" of their patrilineage. Having proven that he is capable of securing the continuation of his line by inseminating a woman and producing a son, a man achieves adulthood and social status. From being a *delikanlı* (unmarried youth, literally "crazy-blooded one"), a man who has channeled his blood through a son becomes a firm link in the chain of generational continuity, empowered like his forefathers to command the respect and total obedience of his family. That is, he becomes a patriarch.

Husbands and Wives: Negotiating Patriarchy

In the classic patriarchal family as it is described by Kandiyoti (1988) and as it appears either as an ideal or in practice among the working-class families of this study, the father, as head of the family, has the final word in all decisions. This does not rule out joint decision making with his wife on, say, purchasing major household items or a car, building a house, or arranging their children's marriages. More often than not, these decisions require a major expenditure of money and therefore the wife's monetary contribution (for example, by selling her gold bracelets) and labor (as in construction) or other assistance, and therefore her goodwill. Nevertheless, this does not obviate the fact that even if the wife disagrees, the husband can still go ahead with the decision, if he is able.

It has been argued that a woman has power or influence even in a patriarchal family, because she has access to information denied a man about such important things as the availability of suitable spouses for their children, and because she controls the household and can wield both her sexuality and the potent weapon of gossip (cf. Rosen 1978, Joseph 1978, el-Messiri 1978).

However, since the father's word carries more weight than all these manners of influence and maneuvers combined, they appear rather to be the tools and weapons of the weak. It might be more accurate to say that a woman's labor and financial strength give her some leverage in family projects.

However, this applies *only* to culturally sacrosanct female wealth such as gold and perhaps to money earned through piecework the exact amount of which the husband has no knowledge. A woman's salary from a regular job is paid directly into the family budget. Sometimes a husband may actually pick up his wife's salary at her place of employment. As one woman told me, "Money is spent more easily than gold." This does not rule out the use of violence, of course. A wife who is not willing to work on construction of their house (I have even heard of pregnant women carrying building materials) or to relinquish her gold bracelets could easily be coerced into changing her mind.

As for information about eligible spouses for their children, a woman's access to such information has more than a purely personal significance only if the family has some wealth and is concerned about economic mergers, or if the family is well connected and wants to make a political union. Since most families do not fall into these categories, mothers try to find grooms with stable employment who will support their daughters, and who will not treat their daughters too badly. Mothers with sons try to find obedient virgin brides from "good families" and with good labor skills.[1]

This is not to say that families are not interested in making alliances with other families which have connections of a sort, such as perhaps an uncle in the civil service, but only that the possibility of such alliances is tempered by a family's own lack of "political" and economic resources. When a possible groom is discussed, preference is given to a man from an economically stable family that is not too distant in origin from the woman's family, if possible from the same family, village, and/or class. Then and only then are the man's personal characteristics and job discussed.

In a *gecekondu* community, brides are often taken (*gelin almak*) from the village from which the family migrated and are usually related (generally first or second degree cousins; but in the village, almost everyone is related to some extent, so the pool of actual marriageable candidates is larger). The reasons given for this custom of taking brides from the village of origin is that the family is known, thus giving the two families certain knowledge about the character and qualities of the prospective bride and groom. If the groom's father owns a small bus company and the groom owns his own bus, this is also an important consideration, because it ensures the economic well-being of the new family and, by implication, brings an extra strand of security into the web of reciprocity that supports the system of related families. Thus, marriage among working-class families is less a matter of political alliance than of weaving a more solid mutual economic base, of diversifying kin assets, so to speak.

It has been suggested that gossip also is a powerful tool which women wield to pursue their aims within the patriarchal family (cf. Joseph 1978). Working-class Cairene women (the Um Belad) have become well known in the literature for their vocalization of perceived injustice (cf. el-Messiri 1978). I believe, however, that gossip plays a slightly different role in Turkey than it does in the Arab world, on which the literature cited above is based.

In Turkey, family problems generally are not discussed outside the family except with close, trusted friends. It is shameful for a woman if it is publicly known that she is not getting along with her husband, that he beats her, and so on, because this reflects on *her* worth. People will think that she has done something to bring this on herself and is perhaps lax in her duties as wife and mother. Since labor, service, and obedience are a part of a wife's identity, if she is beaten for forgetting to sew a button on her husband's shirt, this can be seen as punishment for not being a sufficiently "good" woman. Spreading gossip about one's husband's behavior in Turkey would be self-defeating and bring shame upon the woman.

Kandiyoti (1988) points out that the "patriarchal bargain" struck by Muslim women (such as in Turkey) differs in major respects from that of women in sub-Saharan Africa, also a region characterized by a system of male dominance. In particular, Kandiyoti notes that where the family or household is not perceived as a corporate entity, as in sub-Saharan Africa, in practice women are responsible for their own and their children's upkeep. They therefore try to maximize areas of economic autonomy, such as trading and cultivating their own fields. This allows them to negotiate openly with men the value of their sexual and labor services.

In Muslim communities, on the other hand, women internalize the relations of what Kandiyoti calls classic patriarchy and concentrate their efforts on keeping the patriarchal bargain intact. These communities are characterized by the patrilocally extended household (in practice or as a cultural ideal). Since the bride enters her new home "effectively dispossessed," there are no areas of economic autonomy available to her. Her labor, like her progeny, is appropriated by the patrilineage.

She is subordinate to her husband's family and under the direct authority and control of her mother-in-law. As she grows older and her own son marries, a woman can look forward to gaining control and authority over her own daughter-in-law. Since a son is expected to provide support and security to his mother throughout his life but especially in her old age, women are preoccupied with ensuring their lifelong loyalty. The lack of economic autonomy and the cyclical nature of women's power and authority in the household combine to encourage women to thoroughly internalize this form of patriarchy.

> Thus, unlike women in sub-Saharan Africa who attempt to resist unfavorable labor relations in the household, women in areas of classic patriarchy often adhere as far and long as they possibly can to rules that result in the unfailing devaluation of their labor.... They would rather adopt interpersonal strategies that maximize their security through manipulation of the affection of their sons and husband. (Kandiyoti 1988:280)

As Kandiyoti points out, the potential for women's resistance to oppressive circumstances and the specific forms this resistance takes must be understood within the particular set of concrete restraints that characterize the patriarchal bargain of a given society.

However, within the subset of patriarchal Muslim communities that Kandiyoti describes, there are differences in the counterhegemonic practices available to women. Turkish women, for example, do not have the same access to certain types of manipulation and resistance that are available to their Arab sisters, such as appeal to public opinion to influence intrafamily relations.

Nevertheless, like their Arab sisters, Turkish working-class women attempt to resist economic insecurity primarily by reinforcing their half of the patriarchal bargain—protection and security in exchange for submissiveness and propriety and, I would add, labor.

While Kandiyoti describes this bargain to be primarily between men and women within the family, it could also profitably be seen as a bargain between the individual and the group, of which the conjugal family is a subset. In meeting the moral and labor requirements of her roles as wife, neighbor, mother, and so on, a woman signifies her willingness to participate in the web of reciprocal obligations on which group stability and security (and therefore the security of the individual) rests. Work that is seen to be for individual profit or for individual goals, such as that of the women of sub-Saharan Africa, does not contribute to and therefore does not provide access to group reciprocity.

Men also are expected to contribute their labor to the group. What Kandiyoti calls women's "passive resistance" to men's refusal to live up to their financial responsibilities, I would argue, is in fact an accentuation of the signs of group membership, referring to both family and community, which is the basis for the women's claims to protection and support. By adopting modest behavior and dress and by living up to the requirements of their role in the patriarchal compact, women demonstrate not only to their husbands and sons but to the larger social order that they are members in good standing of that order. They therefore have right of access to the support and protection of the other members, including but not limited to their husbands and sons.

This broader interpretation of women's "passive resistance" does not contradict the notion of a bargain struck between women and men in a patriarchal social order. Rather it attempts to find in the source of empowerment of the patriarchal contract the source of efficacy of this resistance. If the patriarchal contract is seen as a general social contract that links men and women as a group, then women's conservative choices are not only a form of pressure to make men live up to their obligations to their family, but also an accentuation of women's identity as group members, and an appeal to the rules of reciprocity underlying group membership. In other words, if women are members in good standing of the social group, then they are entitled by the rules of group membership to support and security. Social approbation and disapproval are the enforcing factors.

I have heard of cases, however, where men do not support their families, either through chronic unemployment, abandonment, or because they spend much of their earnings on their own entertainment. The implications of the broader view of women's strategies as reinforcing group membership become clear in these cases, since many of these women rely on other members of the group—in-laws or neighbors, for example—to survive. In one case, a young widow with a child began to wear a conservative headscarf in order to remain in favor with her father-in-law so that he would give her money each month. In another case, an old widow whose children provided little support was assisted by her neighbors. Neighborhood women took turns bringing her food, and on religious holidays money was collected and given to her.

The patriarchal order is a pact not only between men and women in marriage but also a set of relations within a wider group which are founded on reciprocity and obligation. The content of these relations of responsibility and obligation and their social configuration (as a patriarchal order) are learned and practiced in the relationship between children and their elders.

Father and Son: Hope and Obedience

The birth of a son is the key to a man's status as patriarch. While the *birth* of a son is of crucial importance to a man, however, his relationship with his son thereafter is often one of formality and restraint, if not tension. A son's major emotional attachment is to his mother.

Generally, sons are spoiled by both parents until the age of seven, when discipline is imparted either through school or through some form of apprenticeship or labor. Sons receive preferential treatment from their mothers, however, throughout their lives. One man, married fifteen years, described coming to his parents' home like this: "My mother treats me like a king from the moment I enter the door. She makes me comfortable, serves me all my favorite foods, and looks after all my needs."

After the age of seven or eight, a son's relationship with his father generally grows formal and constrained, since distance and formalized behavior are signs of respect. Sons also show respect in such ways as not smoking in front of their father. (Girls in any case are expected never to smoke.)

A father provides money for his son's bride-price and wedding expenses. He helps his son to establish himself financially so that he will be able to support a family and thereby continue the patrilineage. He does this either by providing the son with an education or, if he owns a business, by taking his son into it, eventually turning the business over to him. If there are a number of sons, the father may set up branches for each of them. If the father has neither money nor a business, he may use his connections to secure the boy a position as an apprentice to learn a trade. The workshop master becomes the boy's patriarch. The boy owes the master the same loyalty, respect, and total obedience due his father. When handing the boy over to the master, the father traditionally says to him, "The flesh belongs to you, the bones to me."

A son owes his father respect and obedience as well as financial and moral support in his old age. Widowed older men, however, have the option of remarriage. Since remarriage is very difficult for a young woman with children and almost impossible for an older woman, it is more likely that a son will end up looking after an old widowed mother than after his father. The bond between father and son, then, is not as crucial to the father's survival as the mother-son bond is to the survival of the mother.

The combination of the ineluctability of a son's contribution to his father's place in life and the financial and situational options open to the father (such as work and remarriage) lessens the father's dependence on the son. This is in contrast to a mother who, if she has broken relations with her son, may face a poor and precarious old age.[2]

Father and Daughter: Teaching Gender Roles

If the relationship between father and son is one of emotional distance, that between father and daughter is one of propriety and service. As very young children, girls as well as boys may have a more open, affectionate relationship with their fathers. Eventually, however, a girl's relationship with her father and brothers becomes a model for her relationship with men as an adult. She learns to be demure, respectful, and obedient. Since a girl spends most of her time sitting and working with the other women and children of the household and neighborhood, and consequently little time in the male world of her father, responsibility for inculcating proper behavior and attitudes toward men falls to her brother.

A middle-aged man from a traditional urban family, who grew up with three sisters, explains the relationship between father and daughter:

The father is distant, hard to reach (*mesafe*). The mother stands in between. If the children have problems, they go first to the mother, then, if necessary, she passes the problem on to the father.[3] . . . After seven or eight, girls begin to behave more carefully with their fathers, and the father begins to exert great pressure. But relations are different in country and city. In the country, a girl can speak more openly with her father at a later age, so those who come from the country may still have country [relational] patterns although they live in the city.

A girl being more careful with her father means that she learns by behaving toward him how she is supposed to behave with men later. Girl children learn with their fathers that they need to behave more seriously toward men. By seriously, I mean careful, not impertinent (*şımarık*[4]). Because *şımarık* girls are not looked at with a good eye (*iyi gözle bakılmaz*, are disapproved of). People think she's not well brought up. Men think they can sleep easily with such a girl.

In Turkey, in men-women relationships, the important thing is sexuality. The first time a man looks at a woman, he sees first a female, not a person, and adjusts his behavior accordingly. A *şımarık* woman stands too close to a man, touches him while talking, laughs, especially if she laughs like a little girl. This is forbidden at a very early age. The child grows up without even learning to laugh freely. The youths around her say of a young girl who is laughing merrily, "She'll end up a prostitute."

After age seven or eight, a girl begins to behave as a girl is expected to. She doesn't laugh a lot. Her dresses are longer after nine or ten. They cover her knees. After third grade, she may no longer be allowed to go to school because her breasts and hips begin to develop. You don't want her in the same class or on the street with boys. Boys are also taken out of school if their labor power is needed.[5] Also, it's the time for girls to learn housework. The girl is supposed to wait for a husband without having a single stain on her name.[6]

In other words, while a girl's mother teaches her the skills necessary for marriage, her father and brothers are entrusted with teaching and enforcing proper behavior toward men and protecting her honor. Many young girls suffer severe restriction of movement and behavior at the hands of their older brothers, who see this as their duty and may use violence to enforce it.

The different relationships between father and son and father and daughter prepare boys and girls for their future roles in a patriarchal system. Sons learn to respect elder men, but also to demand this respect and obedience from women, girls, and younger children. Their emotional independence from their fathers allows them to establish their own sphere of authority in the future. Daughters, on the other hand, through the behavior required of them toward their father and brothers, learn to be demure, modest, and obedient. This will be the pattern of their future relations with their husbands and their in-laws. From their mothers girls learn the labor skills needed to express these relations.

Reproduction: Of Structure and in Practice

Father and mother provide parallel biological, social, and material systems of reproduction of the family. A father reproduces his bloodline. He assures the normative reproduction of the family (and thereby its place in the larger socioeconomic order), and he supplies the means to satisfy the family's physical needs.

A mother is the soil in which the bloodline is planted. She is the basic incontrovertible medium of biological reproduction. A mother also reproduces family relations moment by moment in practice, supporting the normative order but also continuously creating alternative paths through that order, guiding and supporting her children to their (and her) own goals within the parameters set by her husband and his family and the socioeconomic conditions in which the family is embedded. In addition, she transforms, manages, and distributes the means provided by her husband (and perhaps by herself) to satisfy the family's physical needs.

All phases of a woman's life involve labor and are at the same time sites of material, biological, and social reproduction.[7] In the previous chapters, we have identified three phases of productive activity:

1. A girl's childhood is characterized by the acquisition of social and labor skills which are the keys to marriage (and adulthood). This phase of labor acquisition is associated with (*a*) virginity, the

significant absence of biological reproduction, and (b) engagement and marriage, the pivots of social reproduction.

2. When a woman becomes a wife, her labor becomes an expression of her place within a patriarchal hierarchy. During this phase, she creates her identity as wife, neighbor, "good woman," etc. through labor. This phase is associated with (a) childbearing and (b) the articulation and strategic manipulation of competing social sectors such as the natal and affinal families.

3. When a woman becomes a mother, her labor is invested in her children for her future security. This phase is associated with (a) raising a son and binding him to her emotionally in order to gain leverage within the family and security in her old age and (b) the manipulation of family and social norms (e.g., patriarchal decision making) through financial leverage or through her son for the attainment of personal goals.

During all three phases, a woman contributes to the material reproduction of her own, her husband's, or her natal family. She does this through her labor in the home, that is, by doing housework and possibly by working in a family-owned workshop. She may also do piecework or sell her own products to neighbors or in certain open bazaars, or she may work outside the home.

Motherland, Fatherland

The patriarch protects with strength, provides, administers justice, and demands complete obedience. A mother gives refuge (*barındır-mak*), serves, mediates, and requires emotional loyalty. A similar division of function is reflected in terms referring to the socio-economic order. *Devlet Baba* is "*Father* State" and *Anavatan* is "*Mother* Motherland." Father State is expected to provide for the homeless and the orphaned or fatherless, as well as administer law and justice and provide organization and opportunity for financial advance.[8]

For example, when *gecekondu* houses are razed it is not unusual to hear people raise their voices to Father State, asking him to give them homes. Widows sit outside the district governor's office, waiting to try to "give" their children to Father State to take care of (*sahip çıkmak*). A prisoner escapes from prison and his father gives him up to the authorities saying, "This was my duty to Father State.

Since I did my duty to him, let him be just and not let them torture my son."[9]

The owner of a small piecework atelier complained to me that his atelier was too small to join the artisans' association. When I asked why he didn't get together with other similar ateliers to form an organization of their own, he answered, "The state hasn't created an organization for us." Others apply to Father State to give them jobs, waiting on benches outside the offices of state officials to present their appeals.

Vatan, motherland, on the other hand, is *Anavatan*, "Mother" Motherland. When asked about the difference, one Turk answered, "The state, like God, is a father, is strength. *Vatan* is like a mother; it gives refuge."

Just as in the family the father assures the normative reproduction of traditional family relations, so the Turkish state manages the economy along lines laid down by the liberal economists, raising prices, adjusting interest rates, providing incentives and punishments. Meanwhile, just as the mother in the family reproduces relations moment by moment in practice, the Turkish people renegotiate their material reproduction day by day by acting out norms such as those of reciprocity, steering small amounts of money over and around the systematic channels imposed from above. However, like the position of the wife who is forced to relinquish her gold bracelets to buy a family car, pressure from the patriarchal state empties the pockets of the people in the name of progress. (Ironically, the name of the party in power in the 1980s was the Motherland party (Anavatan Partisi).

Just as a mother saves up the money earned from piecework of which her husband has little knowledge, the citizen (*vatandaş*, "belonging to the motherland") hides income from Father State as insurance against the uncertain future. In both these cases, there is a perceived lack of alternatives, and a consequent adjustment to the situation in daily battle for reproduction at all levels. While upholding in principle the normative and legal order, individuals create alternative paths through that order, be it at the level of untaxed income from home industry or an illegal second job.

The *vatandaş* thereby produces, transforms, manages, and (re)distributes his or her means of material reproduction. In so doing, the *vatandaş* practices strategies of social reproduction that enhance biological continuity. Father State, for its part, is expected to structure society according to law and to uphold the normative order. The "biological" reproduction of the state is by means of nationalism, the *soy* (lineage) of the state. Father State, however, is also expected to provide the means for the physical reproduction of the *vatandaş*—at least by setting a livable minimum wage. This was not the case during the period of my fieldwork, 1986–1988.

Why then do people not revolt even though the state is clearly not assuring (and one might even say is threatening) their material reproduction? While watching news reports about the October 1988 riots in Algeria protesting the high cost of living there, several middle-class Turkish friends ventured the opinion that the Turkish people are sheep. Egypt also was the site of threatened unrest that month, resulting in the rollback by the Egyptian government of planned price increases. Similarities to economic problems in Turkey were obvious.

I would argue that the Turkish people are not sheep, but rather that they see themselves as members of a large family (or group modeled on the patriarchal family) who know their place. If the patriarch fails to provide for their material reproduction, the other family members work together, pooling their labor and meager assets to patch together a strategy for survival day by day. One relatively well-to-do educated friend told me that, despite her advantages, she saw her life and the lives of those around her as a continuous state of crisis management.

Turkish working-class people work as much to fulfil the requirements of a role and to fulfil their duty to family, father, workshop master, or the state as to gain profit.[10] In fulfilling the requirements of their role, individuals place a claim to the collaborative efforts of the group for survival. Survival therefore is seen to be a function of the intensification of traditional role expectations, rather than of their thwarting. Much of the Turkish social and labor system is set up as a hierarchy modeled on the patriarchal family. In a hierarchy, frustration is expressed as downward repression, not as outward resistance.

We have seen in this chapter that labor is intrinsic to relations in the patriarchal family. Men's labor and women's labor provide more than the basis of material reproduction but are also linked, through the ideology of the traditional family, with the social and biological reproduction of the patriarchal family. People's identity as men or as women is expressed and maintained in different ways by their labor contribution to the family (for men, their natal and conjugal family; for women, their conjugal and husband's family; although, as we have seen, this distribution of labor is by no means without conflict).

Thus, men and women in their parental roles each provide in dif-

ferent but parallel ways for the material, biological, and social reproduction of the patriarchal family. Different configurations of labor
characterize each phase of a woman's life as daughter, wife, and
mother, and later, as mother-in-law. These phases are also characterized by contributions to biological reproduction (or its significant
absence through virginity) and to social reproduction as the woman
first learns, then negotiates and teaches patriarchal norms.

In the following chapter I will examine the relationship between
mother and son, the most intense emotional relationship in the
Turkish family, and one in which labor plays a major role in creating
and maintaining the relationship, and in its raison d'être.

Chapter 5
Mothers and Sons

Mother

A young male shopkeeper from a traditional family once told me, "There are two types of Turkish men, the *kılıbık* (henpecked) and the macho.[1] The *kılıbık* does things because his wife wants them done; the macho man does them because his mother wants them." Without doubt, the central relationship in the Turkish family is that between mother and son, regardless of whether the son is married and has a family of his own.

The relationship between mother and son in some way defines and qualifies the other relationships within the family. This chapter looks at how the mother-son relationship acts as a source of identity for men and women, at its role in the biological, social, and material reproduction of the family, and at the importance of labor in creating and maintaining this bond.

A man's mother is his lifelong shadow, sometimes in the background, sometimes in the foreground, but always undeniably present. In other words, men are always "sons of mothers." The word for son, *oğul*, is etymologically related to the word for womb, *oğulduruk*.[2] The word for daughter (*kız*), on the other hand, incorporates a woman's social characteristics with its multiple meanings of daughter, young unmarried girl, and virgin. *Kız* can also be used to refer to a servant, while *oğul* cannot. A man is always a son, but a woman is transformed from *kız* to wife.

The value of children to their parents has been described in the previous chapter. Aside from bringing community respect and adulthood status to both parents, children add complexities of age and gender to the interactions among family members. The relationships between fathers and sons, fathers and daughters, mothers and daughters, and mothers and sons are characterized by different expectations and dynamics. This is due to the different role of each member in the reproduction of the family and to the specific intersection of these roles.

Fathers primarily require the physical existence of children as proof of their manhood (ability to impregnate) and of sons as the continuation of their lineage. They do not require daughters at all.[3] Mothers appreciate daughters for their labor assistance before marriage and may also form close emotional bonds with them. However, due to their precarious structural position and lack of social and economic alternatives, mothers feel that they require sons in order to survive physically and emotionally. This is more of a compelling need than that of the other family members for each other and is reflected in the intensity of the bond a mother forms with her son.

Nurturing Directional Reciprocity

The importance of sons for mothers is reflected in behavior from the day of birth. In some families,[4] when a daughter is born, neighbors are served *şerbet* (flavored sugar water). When a son is born, a nutritious *helva* is made of butter, flour, and sugar and is distributed among friends. I was told that *helva* shows the importance of the event because it is expensive and time-consuming to make. That is, labor is expended differently for boys than for girls from birth. It is primarily through labor (and the unrepayable debt that children incur from it) that mothers attempt to bind their children to them. This is particularly the case for boys, who are from the start recipients of labor in the home, while girls are taught to perform it.

Small children of both sexes, but especially boys, are spoiled and pampered until the age of about seven. There is little or no discipline until then. Children stay awake with their elders until they fall asleep on their own. Then they are carried to bed or left to sleep in the room until everyone else retires.[5] After about age seven, girls begin to do housework and boys learn a trade, or the children go to school.

Girls are taught to obey and serve their fathers and brothers. As they grow older, they take over more and more of their mothers' household labor, and at a very early age they may also begin to contribute labor through piecework, in the family workshop, or in a workshop close by. Any spare time is used by the girls to prepare their trousseaux. Working-class girls are often taken out of school after the third grade in order to preserve their honor (*namus*), which would be threatened in the mixed-gender environment of school. But the girls' labor is generally quickly put to use to earn money or to take over household duties and child care so that their mothers can work. It is a sign of the difficult economic times that in the spring of 1988, young girls of seven or eight began to be seen on the street selling small items (packets of tissues, plastic bags) or standing next to a scale upon which passersby can weigh themselves for a small fee. The street was previously the economic province only of young boys and adults.

Boys, on the other hand, even though they may work under harsh conditions and are treated roughly by their masters, remain "king" in their home. The son continues to be spoiled by his mother, while his relationship with his father becomes more and more formalized and distant (respectful), especially after puberty. The son has complete control over his sister, regardless of her age, and may use violence to enforce it. She, however, is not allowed to strike him back or to retaliate in any way.[6]

I once witnessed a seven-year-old boy beating, cursing, and hurling obscenities at his sixteen-year-old sister (who did nearly all the household chores as well as work in the family workshop). The parents were as usual amused by their son's antics (he treated his two younger sisters, his mother, and even regular female guests in the same manner without being seriously reprimanded). Finally, the usually good-natured girl had had enough and gave her brother a shove to stop him from beating her. The boy released a frustrated, angry shout, and the mother strode up to the girl and slapped her full across the face. No one said a word, and all, including the girl, continued as if nothing had happened.

While obscenity in male children is not acceptable in all families, hitting women (especially sisters) and shouting at them is widely tolerated. Sons are encouraged to demand service and attention from female family members. When a son shouts, a woman almost always answers positively. If she does not respond immediately, a boy shouts until she does.

Women (of all classes and educational backgrounds) serve their sons. A mother peels and slices an apple for her college-age son and takes it to him in his room. Mothers may tie the shoelaces of their sons when they go to high school. If they are in boarding school, the mothers may wash and iron their sheets. This behavior is partly due to the fact that mothers are held to be responsible by society for their children's upbringing and education. However, there is a distinct difference in a mother's labor relation with her male and female unmarried children. Whereas a daughter contributes labor to her mother, a son receives labor from his mother.

As can be expected, patterns established in childhood continue into adulthood. One female friend told me, "Childhood in Turkey never ends. Labor is owed to the parents all one's life. Once when I was around thirty, I heard my father speaking on the phone to someone about his 'child.' It would have been impossible to tell that the 'child' was thirty and married, with a child of its own." A Turkish woman who had returned to Turkey after ten years abroad, expressed her frustration: "Where are the adults?" she exclaimed. "Turks are either children or mothers and fathers!"

In Turkey, a child is always a child, always owes its parents labor and support, but also can expect to be supported by its parents throughout life. It is not surprising that this eternal bond of labor and support expresses itself in all the permutations of the family, the basic social organism. It will also become clear that along with other ideological configurations of labor (such as those discussed in previous chapters), reciprocal relations among family members lend themselves to be harnessed by the capitalist system, either through the provision of cheap products by means of unpaid family labor or through the obligatory "pooling" of family financial and labor resources which cushion survival on a less-than-subsistence wage.

Sons as Security

Women's structural position in Turkish society makes sons crucial to their survival. This is as true today in the cities, if not more so, as it was in the past in the countryside. Despite women's continuous and intensive labor contribution to the family, it is socially preferred for women not to "work," that is to work in waged employment, particularly outside the home.

While unpaid labor is associated with a woman's role identity and "goodness," paid labor is the province of the male. For women, paid labor implies possibly compromising connections with the world outside the home. In 1990 only 15.2 percent of all urban women in Turkey were employed (SIS 1990b). For those women who want to or need to work, job opportunities are scarce for both sexes. Most jobs do not pay enough for an individual to live on one's own, much less support a family alone, even if women were socially permitted to do so.

Thus, if a woman is widowed, or if her husband divorces her, she is generally left without sufficient means of support. Such women who are left with small children and no grown sons often go out to clean houses, leaving the eldest child (usually a daughter) at home to mind the other children. In one case, the eldest daughter was very bright and doing well in school when the father deserted the family to live with another woman. The girl (age fourteen) was taken out of school to watch the four younger children while her mother worked as a cleaning woman.

The mother brings home old newspapers and other reading materials because, she says, "My daughter likes to read." The mother's employer, a professional woman, offered to pay the daughter's school expenses, but since there would be no one to watch the other children, the mother could not accept. (She gave as her reason the fact that her daughter had developed physically and that her honor would be endangered by going to school.) In this case, the daughter was a source of labor. A son would have been a source of income.

When the next oldest girl became old enough to watch her siblings, the oldest daughter began to work as a maid. In times of crisis, girls also are expected to be a source of income. Indeed, the girl's mother is reluctant for her to be married so that she will not lose this crucial extra income.

For her future support, both moral and physical, a woman looks to her son. A son is the ripening fruit of a woman's labor, which binds him to her by means of an enormous debt which can never be repaid.

This sense of indebtedness to one's parents and especially of a man to his mother is commonly and openly expressed, as, for example, when a man chooses to heed the time or labor demands of his mother over those of his wife, explaining, "I can never, never repay everything they did for me." The debt of a child to its mother is also encoded in the "milk debt" (*süt hakkı*[7]), a lifelong debt of service in return for the unrepayable service and sacrifice of the mother, symbolized by breast milk. A mother can curse her son or daughter for disobeying her in a serious matter by saying she will never forgive the "milk debt": "*hakkımı helal etmem.*" This is a severe curse and is never used lightly.

A mother provides for her son physically, emotionally, and if she is able, financially throughout his life. Even mothers who do not "work" use their income from piecework or sell their gold bracelets to meet a son's debt or help him set up in business or get married. A man generally goes to his mother to borrow money, not to his father. The money is not expected to be repaid. (Mothers also lend money to daughters if needed, but this is less common, since the daughter's husband is expected to support her.) Gold is the traditional form in which women save. Their gold bracelets and necklaces are their insurance and security and are not sold lightly. It can be assumed that a son on whom the gold is spent is an even better source of security.

Constructing Ties That Bind Mother and Son:
Religion and Eroticism

Mothers go to great lengths to tie their sons to them emotionally. This is by no means an unconscious process, since women are well aware of their structural vulnerability and their limited options for security. A mother explained to a fellow mother at school: "I want my son to get an Islamic education, so I'm sending him every Friday to prayers at the mosque. In this way, he won't leave his mother." "Of course," she added grudgingly, "he will also be concerned with his wife, but he'll never leave me." Ironically, this woman is plagued by an unpleasant mother-in-law and suffers from migraine headaches that an acquaintance suggested are related to this.

In uncertain economic times, when average people have no savings and no security, any means that are seen to strengthen family ties flourish. Since Islam stresses responsibility to one's parents, parents may be more likely to use it (in the above case quite openly) to bind their children (and their children's future income) to them.

The relationship between mothers and sons has many ties that bind them. A sense of erotic attachment (which alludes to desire without reference to the sexual act itself) can be discerned in their interaction. A mother seated on the bus before me plays with her grown son's hair and ear. A mother and her teenage son sit entwined like lovers on the ferry, not disentangling even when they get up to disembark. A professional woman casually repeats to her young son over and over in the office of a friend they are visiting, "I'm your big passion, your only love, aren't I? You'll never leave me, isn't that right?"

The industrialist Sakıp Sabancı, in an interview on television, was asked what his favorite activity was when traveling. He reportedly answered that his favorite pastime is to travel to Europe with his mother and to stay in the same hotel room: "Then I feel like I am with Sophia Loren."

The Turkish friend (a professional woman) who related this incident to me thought it was very funny and repeated it to some European friends. After she told the story, she said, there was a pause and finally one man said, "Weird." She was a bit startled that they hadn't seen the humor. "Incest," I explained quietly, "is not funny in the West." These, she insisted, are considered in Turkey to be the feelings of a model son toward his mother.

In one family I stayed with, the seven-year-old son reached at will into his mother's sweater and played with her breasts,[8] sometimes accompanying this with obscene hand gestures aimed indiscriminately at whoever was in the room. Although boys of that age are still said to be children and are tolerated in the presence of naked women, for example at a public bath (unless they are physically well developed), they are also at that age taught sexual behavior and attitudes toward women by their male relatives. This same seven-year-old child let out a wolf whistle and made an obscene gesture when a buxom blonde in a bikini appeared on the video screen.

Boys up to age seven (or occasionally older if they are not physically well developed) may spend hours with their mothers in the presence of naked and half-naked women in beauty-treatment salons and at the public bath (*hamam*).[9] When they are older, I am told by male friends, men sometimes relate these experiences to each other in crude humorous terms, as in describing the size of a woman's breasts and buttocks, the appearance of female genitalia, or activities such as removing pubic hair.

In Figure 1, a young boy goes to the public bath to have one arm scrubbed, has the barber put cologne on it, then dries it in the sun. Afterward he presents the arm to his mother's female guest, who gives him permission to feel her breast now that his hand is clean and warm. In Figure 2, the boy is sent into paroxysms of excitement at the sight of his mother's female guests' disarranging their clothing because of the heat. The boy, Avni, is a very well known and popular cartoon character in Turkey, much loved for his boyish pranks. In scene 1 of Figure 3, a young boy sits among a group of women who have come together for their social "day." The women illustrate their conversation about depilation (of legs and genital region) and medical diagnoses by showing the relevant parts of their bodies. Scene 2 shows the boy years later as a man in a coffeehouse telling his companions a lewd account of what he saw that day. At the same time, he refers to the women as "aunt" or "elder sister," terms of familiarity and respect.

I was told it is not culturally acceptable for men to speak to each other about women from an emotional or even erotic point of view.[10] Men who try to describe their own arousal or erotic reactions are thought to be lying or exaggerating. Such topics are considered "romantic" or sensitive (*hassas*) and are off limits to discussion under threat of ridicule. "Women," as one male friend put it, "are only to be fucked. That's the way they are talked about."

In other words, while young boys are aware of and exposed early to the world of sex and women, this world is partitioned off at a very early age from the realm of emotional relations with women. This partitioning, perhaps, is an attempt to deal with the initial associa-

Panel 2
—You've honored our bath, Avni. Come, let me scrub you . . .
Panel 3
—Why wash only one arm?
Panel 5
—Why cologne only on the left arm?
Panel 6
—What's he doing?
—Warming his arm in the sun.
Panel 7
His mother's guest:
—So this time it's clean, nice smelling, and not like ice.
OK, if that's so, I give you permission.

Figure 1. From *Girgir* 815:15, April 17, 1988.

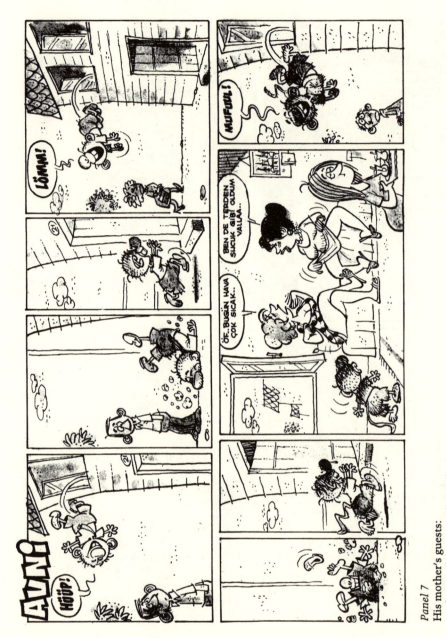

Figure 2. From *Girgir* 828:15, July 17, 1988.

Panel 7
His mother's guests:
—The weather is very hot today.

Figure 3. From *Girgir* 832:11, August 14, 1988.

Panel 1
—There was a lump in my breast, but nothing serious developed.
—The salon did a great job of depilation (waxing).
—My dear, I told them to wax farther up and it's bruised.

Panel 2
—Uff. I still can't forget "Aunt" Shahsane's breasts. Like melons. Afterward "Sister" Hülya raised her skirt and showed where they had waxed.
—I told you then that we shouldn't bring the children to the women's social day.

tion of a boy's awareness of women's sexuality with his feelings toward his mother. The unspoken naked woman's body next to those women's bodies spoken of in sexual terms, after all, is that of the man's mother.

Sexual satisfaction effectively becomes separated from emotional satisfaction, including erotic feelings which are perceived to be intimate, sensitive, emotional, and generally divorced from sex. Sex is an activity engaged in with one's wife and with women not identified with family roles. I was told by two gynecologists who worked in the major birthing hospital (used almost exclusively by working-class women), one of whom had also practiced medicine for a few years in a village in eastern Turkey, that many working-class men had never seen their wives' bodies naked above the waist and that sex for a married couple tended to revolve around the simple physical satisfaction of the man and contain little or no erotic arousal for the woman.[11]

In other words, sex can be seen as taking place between men and women for the satisfaction of men's physical need and as being itself relatively empty of emotional content. The feelings between a mother and her son, on the other hand, are intensely charged and have an erotic component (which is, however, empty of sexual content). This association of eroticism with the sacrosanct emotions of love for one's mother makes any public discussion of erotic behavior or arousal off limits, since this is an intimate and private matter that should not be put on public display. As Delaney points out (1991a: 174) Fatima Mernissi's comments about Moroccan society are also applicable to Turkey in this regard. The son's love for his mother "is not a process with a beginning, a middle and a ritualized end, indicating that now the adult male can engage in a new heterosexual relationship with his wife. . . . Marriage institutionalizes the Oedipal split between love and sex in a man's life. He is encouraged to love a woman he can't engage in sexual intercourse with, his mother. He is discouraged from lavishing his affection on the woman he does engage in sexual intercourse with, his wife" (1975:69–70).

For the sake of devoting herself to her children, a widow may give up sexual activity, the companionship of a husband, and male support (although this is traditionally provided by the husband's family). This means she also gives up a varied social life, particularly if she is young and lives in the city. Except for visits to all-women *kabul* social gatherings, a lone woman's social life is curtailed. She is considered a threat to other women's husbands, and she must keep her own honor spotless. This is less of a problem in more traditional neighborhoods where most women's activities are segregated and becomes more of a problem in middle-class urban culture where visiting among families is gender mixed.

I mentioned these problems to Ayşe, who is herself remarried with two children, one by her previous husband. Ayşe responded, "It would be unthinkable for a Turkish woman to even say, much less think, that she would like something for herself (a career, self-gratification of any sort, companionship, and so on) and to put that above dedication to her child. The only possible reason to get remarried is a financial reason. And that is also directly related to the well-being of the child."

The end result of these emotional strategies is to keep the man an eternal child (see Figure 4). In 1987 an advertisement for an oven appeared on Turkish television showing a happy young son saying, "Now we have an electric oven!" while his mother fed her husband with a fork as if he were a child. A mother's labor and service to her son is expected from the wife as well. Husbands can expect their wives to awaken them in the morning, to lay out their clothing and prepare their breakfast, in addition to doing all the other service and labor tasks involved in running the household.

The son's labor, on the other hand, is an arena of battle, with wife and mother making competing claims. Wives often complain that

"8 Mart Kadınlar Günü"

Figure 4.
From *Cumhuriyet*,
March 8, 1988.

"8 Mart Kadınlar Günü"

"March 8 Women's Day"

their husbands spend too much time at their parents' homes or that when the wife needs something done, the mother-in-law invariably calls and requires her son's labor for that day, "almost as if it were on purpose." His mother's claim usually takes precedence over that of his wife for a man's time and labor.

In Chapter 3, I discussed the battle between a woman's natal family and her husband's family over control of her labor. A similar battle is fought between a man's mother and wife over his time and labor. Women in their various roles battle to tie to them with secure personal bonds of love, guilt, and duty the labor which forms the bedrock of their material security. Mothers usually but unwillingly relinquish their daughters' labor and income when these marry. The bride's labor is important to the mother-in-law for the same reasons, especially as she grows older.[12] A *gelin*'s labor, like that of a daughter, can also provide income to the family through piecework or by supplying household labor while the mother-in-law works. The most important and enduring source of income, however, is a son.

In her battle over the important resource that is her son, the mother has contradictory expectations of the *gelin* with regard to children. On the one hand, the mother-in-law expects the *gelin* to have a male child to fulfill her son's expectations of status and adulthood and her husband's for continuation of the patrilineage. On the other hand, a child, especially a son, binds the mother-in-law's son closer to his wife (the *gelin*), gives the wife status, thus decreasing the mother-in-law's control over the woman's labor, and legitimately takes the wife's attention away from labor duties to the mother-in-law while she takes care of her own child. Thus, while a mother-in-law will vilify a *gelin* who does not promptly produce a son, one also hears of mothers-in-law who resent a *gelin*'s pregnancy, try to take the baby from her after it is born (if the mother-in-law lives separately), or mistreat mother and child.

The mother-in-law is forced to relinquish the biological reproduction of the family to the *gelin*. However, for her own survival, she must bind the labor (and income) of her son to herself. In other words, she must make certain that the material reproduction of her son's family includes her own (and her family's) reproduction. She does this by attempting to deny the function of social reproduction to the *gelin*, limiting her to the biological and material reproduction of the family.

That is, the mother-in-law attempts to retain control over the daily practice of family life (including that of her son's family). She does this by supporting the authority of the father (her husband) and of her son, thereby placing herself in the position of being able to negotiate with or through that authority. One language in which these relations and battles are expressed is that of labor expected and demanded, labor given and denied, and labor transferred and contested.

Labor within the family is both a source of self-identity and resistance, and a means of finding and binding security in the form of children. Relations among family members are at one and the same time relations of self-realization and of exploitation. However, because of women's socioeconomic insecurity, this seemingly contradictory pairing particularly characterizes relations between mother and son and between mother-in-law and *gelin*.

The position or role of mother or mother-in-law generally has been treated in the literature as part of the continuous life cycle of an individual who rises in status with each successive phase of her life (cf. Kandiyoti 1988). I have argued here that the individual woman as an abstract concept (except as sexual object) is alien to the Turkish view of the individual as member of a defining group. Therefore I believe that one must look at the position of mother or mother-in-law as being embedded within a particular harmony (or disharmony) of relations that is the family. Every mother has her own mother, a husband, a mother-, father-, and sister-in-law, and children, probably of both sexes. A mother-in-law has a husband, son, other children (such as daughters), as well as a *gelin* with her children, and perhaps in-laws of her own.

Each configuration of this harmony strikes a different note depending on the socioeconomic context and objective conditions within which the needs and strategies of the members are defined. So far, I have traced the different notes and observed that an underlying unifying theme is that of labor—labor given, labor expected, labor received or denied. What follows in the next chapter is an attempt to trace the same theme (labor as both self-realization and exploitation) along similar trajectories within the harmony (or disharmony) of the Turkish socioeconomic system.

Chapter 6
The Social Web

İyilik yap
Denize at
Balık görmezse
Halik görür

(Do a favor
Throw it into the sea;
If the fish don't see it
the Creator will.)

—A Turkish saying

Gentle Violence

It has been shown in the previous chapter that the exploitation of labor in the Turkish family occurs along lines of socially defined relations of domination and subordination. One of the ways in which these relations of domination are internalized is through socialization, a learning of the association between relations of labor and definition of the self. In this chapter, I will argue that the ideological construction of labor as social identity (as modeled by relations within the family) and the relations of domination which this construction misrepresents also underlie economic behavior in Turkey outside the family.

The ideology of labor is a mythical structure that makes relations of domination and exploitation seem a "natural" part of social life in Turkey. At the same time, it provides the means for a long-term survival strategy within and around sets of institutions and material conditions that cannot be relied on to ensure reproduction of the basic social unit, the family.

The practical success of this scheme of perception and thought that makes up the cultural understanding of labor in Turkey contributes to its reproduction through socialization and to its naturalization under new material conditions such as those that have come about since the 1970's. Relations of domination that are learned and expressed within this ideology of labor are thereby transplanted (or grafted) to new economic conditions involving capitalist markets and other forms of exploitation.

In Turkey relations of domination and exploitation within the family, within the workshop, and in economic and social transactions in general are euphemized as purely personal (although not necessarily individual) relations through which no profit is obtained by anyone, but rather labor, money, and time are freely given and no immediate return is expected. The concept of the gift is thereby used to misrecognize debts, moral and monetary. Rather than seeking closure through countergifts, people try to keep relations open-ended—that is, to remain indebted. Both reciprocity and indebtedness are expressed and codified as social and religious moral imperatives.

According to Bourdieu, the euphemization of domination as positive social relations is particularly characteristic of precapitalist economies because these economies lack sufficient institutions to ensure the interests of the dominant class (1979:189). In the absence of institutions or other objective mechanisms of domination, continuous conscious effort must be expended to reproduce unequal relations. For this reason, domination is direct, person to person, accomplished through the forging of bonds which appear to have positive social content.

Bourdieu calls this "symbolic violence, the gentle, invisible form of violence, which is never recognized as such, and is not so much undergone as chosen, the violence of credit, confidence, obligation, personal loyalty, hospitality, gifts, gratitude, piety—in short, all the virtues honoured by the code of honour" (ibid.:192). This hidden violence does not obviate overt physical and economic violence but coexists with it.

> This coexistence of overt physical and economic violence and of the most refined symbolic violence is found in all the institutions characteristic of this economy, and at the heart of every social relationship . . . with the "choice" between overt violence and gentle, hidden violence depending on the relative strengths of the two parties at a particular time, and on the degree of integration and ethical integrity of the arbitrating group.
> (Ibid.:192–193)

Collective reprobation, or community censure, is another means by which overt violence ("the violence of the usurer or the merciless master") is discouraged in favor of gentle violence.

The active principle in the transformation of the overt domination of a disinterested relationship into the socially recognized domination of legitimate authority is "the labour, time, care, attention, and savoir-faire which must be squandered to produce a personal gift irreducible to its equivalent in money . . . the seemingly 'gratuitous' surrender not only of goods or women but of things that are even more personal and therefore more precious, . . . such as *time*. . . . The exercise of gentle violence demands a *'personal'* price from its users" (ibid.).

In other words, personal authority based on gentle violence must be continuously reaffirmed in practice through strategies involving giving and receiving. Giving, Bourdieu writes, is also a way of possessing. If a gift is not matched by a countergift, it creates a lasting bond and restricts the freedom of the receiver (ibid.:195). Both the gift and the debt, "in spite of their apparent opposition, have in common the power of founding either dependence . . . or solidarity, depending on the strategies with which they are employed" (ibid.:192). In this chapter, I will show how socially valorized indebtedness underlies economic practice in Turkey and creates, maintains, and naturalizes relations of domination and exploitation.

In Turkey institutions and a polity are in place that ensure the reproduction of a small dominant class; however, the reproduction of social and economic relations of domination in society as a whole is secured by institutions and social mechanisms which operate on the basis of continual personal investment in the establishment and maintenance of power. The state is itself an uncertain institution, especially from the standpoint of economic stability, with civil violence always threatened and military takeovers occurring every ten years on average.

Relations of domination based on the gentle violence of obligation and reciprocity, on the other hand, appear reliable for long-term commitment and flexible in the face of unforeseen events. In the Turkish family, relations of domination such as those between mother and son are reproduced through the accumulation of unrepayable indebtedness in the name of love, simultaneously ensuring the mother's long-term economic security.

In the same way, family members contribute wages or unpaid labor to the family so that it can continue to survive in a hostile economic environment. Such labor is at the same time a conscious contribution to the economic security of the family and an unconscious expression of each individual's identity as a family member. As a result, while acknowledged as a contribution to the family's economic welfare, family labor is not thought of as work (in the sense of work for pay, or alienated labor).

In the sector of the economy, then, that is based primarily on family and neighborhood labor, economic relations and the relations of domination inherent in them, like relations within the family, are misrecognized as relations of personal dependence, obligation, and reciprocity. This mostly unconscious orchestration of power relations is also accompanied by overt economic violence.[1] However, as Bourdieu points out, "the strategies of symbolic violence are often ultimately more economical than pure 'economic' violence" (ibid.: 190).

A necessary attribute of that sector of the Turkish economy based on the "enchanted relationships" of gentle violence is that work is done more for status and security than for profit. The desire for profit is a naked economic motive undeniably present in economic relations. In order to reproduce relations of domination in the sector of the economy based on family and neighborhood labor, the profit motive must be misrecognized. Family relations provide a metaphor for this. This is not to say that there is no desire for increased fortune, or greed or envy. Rather, these motivations are directed toward the enhancement of security and status, rather than toward monetary gain for its own sake. This will be discussed in the following chapters with particular reference to the organization of piecework labor.

Economic relations in Turkish society are euphemized as reciprocal social bonds on a wider scale than only among those involved in small production. Unspoken (because necessarily unconscious) rules of social exchange and reciprocity regulate even the exchange of money for a purchase in what would appear to be a simple and naked economic transaction.

The use of telephones, fax machines, and increasingly, computers in business does not obviate the importance of face-to-face interaction. The strategies of debt and exchange which are at the root of symbolic domination require physical presence for the manipulation of space and time (and timing), and in order to bring to bear personal attributes such as hospitality and shared social connections. The importance of social over economic relations makes Turkish business highly resistant to the depersonalization through automation that characterizes business in the West.

To sum up, for most people with limited resources the vagaries of Turkish economic and political life do not provide a climate for long-term economic growth based on risk or investment. This is compounded by the fact that conditions of the "naked" labor market are not conducive to survival, much less growth of the family or business. The individual or group, then, relies on different strategies for ensuring security and growth. In these strategies for growth and security, relations of domination (and their expression in labor) within the family act as a metaphor for relations of domination (and economic action) within society.

Personal Business

The portly gray-haired owner of the tiny used-book store stood in the narrow space left by the two occupied chairs and the desk. A young assistant with a pleasant round face stood in the doorway. Georg, a book buyer for a German scholarly institute, was interested in buying some books. The visit took all afternoon. We drank tea, brought in small tulip-shaped glasses on a tray from a nearby tea stand that served the shops. The owner talked about his children and asked Georg when his family was coming to visit. As they were talking, the assistant would reach up occasionally to a shelf, as if an afterthought, pull out a volume, hand it to Georg or to me, and murmur, "You might be interested in this." The personal conversation would go on while Georg or I perused the proferred volume. Some very interesting books appeared, which I either added to a stack on the desk or handed back, all at a very leisurely pace.

The owner took us to lunch in the nearby covered bazaar. We sat and talked again, mostly about events in his personal life: his recent diet, his young daughter's mischief, and her jealousy of the family's new baby. We also talked about neutral topics such as food and other foreign scholars that patronize the shop. The owner paid the bill, although we didn't see him do so.

Back in the shop, the process of having a personal conversation while doing business unobtrusively began again. After two hours, Georg indicated his quite substantial stack of books and said that this would be all for the time being. Still, no one changed what they were doing, except that the serendipitous finding of relevant books decreased. A short, red-headed apprentice appeared in the slanting late-afternoon light of the doorway and was dispatched to get a vehicle from their warehouse, to give us a ride. The information about Georg's destination was elicited in a roundabout manner which bespoke more of an interest in his activities that day.

Money was hardly ever mentioned except when the book was very old and expensive, in which case it was mentioned lightly, often in the context of a story about the book in question or the high prices of books from certain publishers. Being on a limited budget, I felt clumsy having to ask the price of each book I was interested in. I tried to do it unobtrusively, but felt embarrassed nevertheless.

When five o'clock approached and I felt sure the vehicle would appear at any moment, I became concerned that there would be no time to write up and pay for my books, so I suggested that maybe we could make out a receipt for my books. The owner and assistant answered, "Of course," and did nothing. I realized it was unnecessary to worry about there not being enough time—there is *always* enough time here. Another half hour passed. Georg's books had been written up and packaged slowly during the course of the afternoon. They were not mentioned; no money changed hands; no final amount was announced. The bill was tucked in with the books. Georg would pay it later after getting the approval of his institute. We sat chatting in the dimming afternoon light filtering in from the door, waiting for the car.

I found myself getting edgy about paying. At one point, I moved my pile of books into the center of the desk. After a while, the owner glanced at them briefly, stating in general, "You wanted to buy these" (*almak* means "to buy" as well as "to take," adding ambiguity to his statement) as if that took care of the matter, then continued his conversation about other matters. A few minutes later, the assistant wrote up a receipt and I took out the money, 50 TL[2] over the amount. I put it in the middle of the desk, where it was pointedly ignored by everyone. The owner glanced at it briefly, probably to see if change was needed. The conversation meandered along other topics. After a while, I became embarrassed at the money lying like an open sore in full view and moved it to the side of the desk on top of a pad of paper.

Only when the car had come and we had said our farewells and were walking out of the shop did I see the assistant scoop the money into the desk drawer. The receipt had been given to me before, while we were talking about other things. No one expressed the least interest in my money. The fact that no one gave me the 50 TL change indicates, I believe, that this minor infraction was secondary to the major goal of keeping business out of business.

This is the tenor of most business conducted in Turkey: face-to-face, it involves an investment of time, certain personal information, service, and hospitality. It is, however, business, and along with the gentle economic violence of personal bonds, is an expectation of payment.

An old man came into Murad's electric shop in a working-class neighborhood on the European shore of the Bosphorus. He gave Murad a fishing net he had repaired for him. As the man turned to leave, he asked Murad to give him a length of electrical wire. He didn't pay but Murad told him the price as he walked out the door. I asked Murad if the wire was in exchange for fixing the net. He was scandalized: "Is such a thing possible?! He buys a lot of stuff on credit and pays once a month." Reciprocity, I learn, is never immediate and cannot be seen to be measured payment for a measured service. Reciprocity by nature is open-ended. Otherwise, it is business. Murad thought it outrageous to even consider payment for a (reciprocal) service like fixing a net.

Since business transactions in Turkey often lack the markers we associate with business in the West—prices, money, impersonal service, immediate or scheduled payment—it is easy to confuse business with reciprocal relations. Both appear to be personal relations bound up with sets of mutual obligations (I feel guilty if I patronize a different bookseller). Such business transactions have elements of continuity as a result of the gentle economic violence that secures long-term clientele through an indebtedness not related to money.

Business relations differ from nonbusiness reciprocal relations perhaps only in terms of ultimate closure. Business transactions are in one respect temporally complete—selection is followed by payment, even if not immediate, at least within a specified time. Otherwise the relation is endangered; time, services, and credit may be withdrawn. Reciprocal relations depend on lack of closure. Hospitality, labor, services are donated. As Bourdieu points out (1979: 183), while return is expected, it cannot be a conscious expectation.

This contradiction of business relations requiring closure while also—as reciprocal relations—requiring open-endedness is resolved (or at least hidden) by the studious avoidance of dwelling on economic symbols such as money or bills of sale during the transaction. However, the difference, as Murad demonstrated, is clear to everyone. Blending the boundaries by being too personal in business relations or by being too business-like in personal relations is frowned upon.

For example, a person's close friend (or close family member) who owns a shop is expected to sell to them at cost. Therefore, it is not considered proper to patronize the shop of a close friend, at least too often, because it is financially ruinous to them. As one middle-class woman put it: "If an item is over a certain amount, you'd rather buy it off a shark and lose money than buy it off a relative . . . because you wouldn't want a relative to lose that much because they couldn't make a profit off you."

Profit

There are gradations in the amount of profit allowed and the extent to which the business content can be openly expressed over the reciprocal content of a transaction. These gradations are based on the degree of closeness of the partners in the transaction. Degree of closeness is not necessarily measured in structural terms such as kinship proximity, although this may be an important element, but rather is an expression of a reciprocal debt already built up which has been continually renewed over a period of time. The reciprocal content of such transactions must appear paramount.

For many months it puzzled me that the young vegetable-shop owner in my neighborhood, with whom I also visited to chat socially in his shop, insisted that I pay for my purchases at a later time (*"sonra ver,"* give [it] later), when I already had the money in my hand at that moment. (Like *al*, which means both "buy" and "take," *ver* means both "pay" and "give," making the business content of his request ambiguous.) At first I refused and pressed the money on him because I was afraid that I might forget the amount that I owed him and because I felt that if he wouldn't let me pay for my purchases, I would be too embarrassed to shop there anymore. It took a long time to overcome my anxiety over what I perceived from my own perspective to be an intrusion of the personal side of our relationship on the business side, thereby endangering the latter. It was only when I noticed the same behavior—almost begging me to pay later—on the part of other shopkeepers with whom I had a personal relationship that I realized its significance. By putting off payment, the open-ended (reciprocal and therefore personal) nature of the relationship was highlighted.

The emergence of money and profit too close to the surface of the transaction/relation causes anxiety. The introduction (or recognition) of a naked profit motive may endanger or even end the relationship. If it is necessary for money to change hands between friends or relatives, it must be done accurately and personally, with no apparent profit on either side by giving too much or too little.

Since I had brought too little money with me, Olcay, a close friend with whom I was staying for a few weeks, paid the equivalent of forty dollars in lira for some clothing I purchased in a shop. At home, I asked her, rather awkwardly, if she would prefer to have the money in dollars, arguing that I would anyway only change dollars at the bank to give her liras. (Foreign currency is a favorite hedge against the steadily devalued lira.) She agreed but impressed upon me that there was no hurry for repayment. The next day, I placed fifty dollars on the dresser in her bedroom, since I was also going to make an international telephone call. That evening, since she didn't mention it, I remarked that I had put the money on the dresser. "Yes," she said shortly, "I saw it. *Ayıpsın* [You are shameful, unmannerly]," and left the room. Embarrassed, I followed her to the kitchen and hastily explained that the other ten dollars was for a telephone call. "We'll find out how much it costs first," she said curtly and changed the subject. At breakfast the next morning, she handed me the money without a word. I said nothing but went that day to the post office to check the telephone charges, and made my call that evening. After figuring out the exact amount I owed her, I gave it to her and said, "Thanks." She put the money away and that was the end of the matter. In my fieldnotes that evening, I wrote, "Rule: Never try to give people money unless agreed upon first, then in their hand."

Asuman, a middle-class schoolteacher, selected two carpets from a shop she has patronized for over twenty years. She left a deposit of 20,000 TL (about $27). She took the carpets home to try them out, then brought one of the carpets back along with a sack of old carpets as partial payment for the carpet she had decided to keep. She paid the balance in cash.

A few days later, she realized that the shopkeeper had figured the cost of the carpet she kept, minus the price for the sack of old carpets, but had forgotten to subtract the deposit. She telephoned him and reminded him of the deposit. He was horrified and angry at himself, Asuman relates, and she wished she had just forgotten about it. He wanted to send someone immediately in a cab from the other side of the city to give her the money. Asuman insisted she would come herself in a few days. As soon as she entered the shop, the owner's brother slipped her the money. It was not mentioned aloud and Asuman did not count it. (Counting money or checking the bill in a transaction between people who share a reciprocal relationship must be done either in a straightforward but unobtrusive manner or not at all. Under certain circumstances, counting money can be considered rude or even insulting. This reluctance to verify the transaction when it occurs easily leads to errors such as the one described above.)

What is said and not said about the business aspect of a transaction, then, can cause anxiety and shame and can be misconstrued as an insult. Talking about or disputing money openly implies that the relationship has closure and is therefore business only as between strangers. Time is a crucial element; if payment is immediate, the transaction loses any social value because the reciprocity on which social relations rest can be neither created nor maintained.

This is not the case with a gift (present, *hediye*), which is often immediately reciprocated, to show that it is appreciated. This is much to the dismay of the Western gift-giver in whose own culture gifts must be returned after an interval of time has elapsed, so as not to give the impression that one gift "buys" the other. What is exchanged in a reciprocal relation in Turkey are not gifts (presents), but debts—the indebtedness calling forth feelings of guilt and obligation to cement both a sense of solidarity (as family, friends, acquaintances, nonstrangers) and dependence. It is not surprising that the giving of gifts (as in the sense of a birthday or anniversary present) is not common in Turkey, given the widespread and continuous circulation of goods and labor that characterizes the society.

Van Baal (1975), in his critical review of theories of the gift, argues that while goods exchanged as gifts aim to strengthen social bonds, the goal of trade is fundamentally different. The goal of trade is a balanced reciprocity of direct exchange, although with the possibility of delayed requital. Trade, in this view, is impersonal, ideally balanced, and a matter of bargaining rather than an exchange of gifts, the parties dispersing afterward without any further obligation to one another (ibid.:39). Extrapolating from the difference between *gimwali* trade in the Trobriand Islands and other forms of Trobriand exchange, he writes, "Even in the case of traders who deal regularly with each other (not uncommon in economically more advanced societies) the relationship remains commercial, distinct from the personal ties that may have developed in the course of prolonged contacts."

Trade, however, may be facilitated by being associated with or situated within a ceremonialized environment that assures peace and increases contacts. "The occasion to trade, if it does not present itself by chance, must be purposively created" (ibid.:42). Van Baal gives the example of the institution of trade-friendship in New Guinea, where trade-friends are "like relatives," exchange presents, and help each other acquire desired commodities. "The trade-friendship is a mutual gift-relation that promotes opportunities for commercial barter" (ibid.).

According to Van Baal, then, trade differs fundamentally from gift-exchange (although the latter can function to facilitate the former) in that trade "does not have, nor is it meant to have a unifying effect" (ibid.:43), whereas the purpose of gift-exchange is to establish or strengthen a relation between the persons making the exchange. Trade relations in Turkey as described above, however, evince a more intrinsic link between the development of social relations through reciprocity and the exchange of commodities through bargaining. The giving of personal information and assistance, time, and tea, as well as the insistence on paying later, are all aimed at developing social bonds, along with their attendant reciprocal obligations. I argue that this search for open-ended reciprocity, even in what is clearly understood to be trade (with ultimate closure), is not merely designed to enhance the loyalty of customers or to facilitate trade. Rather, trade relations, like all reciprocal relations, foster the social solidarity and mutual dependence that are the bedrock of Turkish social identity and that provide strategies for survival. This is nowhere more clearly illustrated than by the association of basic elements of trade, such as profit, with religious and cultural ideals of social justice.

Money Is Justice

The notion of profit is intricately bound up with the complex choreography of business/reciprocal relations. "Money is justice [*hak*]," a young shopkeeper pointed out to me. Illicit gain is therefore unjust. "If someone does some work and, instead of 1,000 TL, takes 1,500, thereby gaining excessive earnings, it is injustice to you. But if the price is negotiated beforehand, it's OK to make a greater profit." This notion is closely tied to his religious beliefs. "*Helâllık* [canonically legitimate]: To take excessive pay [*ücret*] for your labor is *haram* [forbidden by religion]. You'll get punished after death."

The focus of the shopkeeper's explanation was not on how much of a profit would be considered excessive but on keeping to what the profit was understood to be. A lawful profit is that which is agreed upon; a forbidden profit is one which is in excess of what was agreed upon. Emphasis is on the social agreement rather than on the market value of the product or labor. There exists a subtle sliding scale, as described above, of what profit is lawful, ranging from the understood proscription of profit among close friends, through various reductions in price depending on the relation's reciprocal foundation, to the more or less open negotiation of price among strangers or near strangers.

Olcay complained bitterly one evening about her friend, a dentist, who she said had overcharged her for her bridge. She has known him for a long time, and over ten years ago they had shared an office, a common practice among professionals who cannot afford an office on their own. She said he had told her he would only charge her for materials, but that he had badly overcharged her for them. He charged her more than 200,000 TL (about $265) for what, according to another dentist friend, could not have been more than 90,000 TL

($120) of materials (gold). She felt betrayed and said she could never go to see him anymore because of this.

To recapitulate, then, when close friends or relatives conduct business, the "buyer" sometimes does not expect to pay at all, thus denying the business aspect altogether, or the item is sold at cost. If it is an expensive item, the buyer may choose to purchase it elsewhere so as not to cause a financial loss to the friend. With this degree of closeness, then, business *is* reciprocity.

Among friends or relatives without such close and continually renewed ties, the buyer expects and is given an automatic reduction in price, so that the profit is minimal. In such relationships, one partner may claim fictive kinship, saying that the other is "my niece," "my paternal uncle," and so on, depending on age and gender. This is different from the metaphoric use of kin terms such as brother, elder brother, elder sister, paternal uncle, and maternal aunt, which is common throughout the society and can occur between strangers as signs of respect.

Business relations at a slightly greater personal remove, say between a regular customer and a shop owner, may involve bargaining "secretly" to reduce the price. The maneuvering to lower the price (which is common and expected in most business transactions) takes place under cover of personal conversation and over glasses of tea. While the price is openly mentioned and negotiated, this is done within the format of a social visit and seems on the surface to play a minor role in the visit. The end price is expected to be significantly lower than the starting price, although it is assumed that the shop owner will still make a profit.

At the level of business relations between strangers or near strangers, it is assumed that the seller will try to obtain the highest profit possible and the buyer will try to negotiate using, among other strategies, that of searching for and bringing forth reciprocal ties based on such things as common place of origin, distant relations, friends or acquaintances in common, similarity in experiences, school ties, or whatever the buyer can find to establish a modicum of connection upon which a reciprocal edifice can be built. Even among near strangers, however, naked economic motives often remain hidden.

Business relations, then, permit—indeed require—certain gradations of personal interest. Personal relations permit only a very limited range of business-like behavior (that is, economically oriented behavior with closure).

Asuman says that her aunt and cousin are a scandal to the family and a constant cause of reproving talk. Both are "penny-pinching" types. If the (married) daughter goes to her mother's house and brings her a cake which the mother had asked her to bring, she says, "Well, mother. I paid so-and-so much for this cake. *Haydi bakalım* [All right, let's see (the money)]." This requiring and giving of money in the family shocks the other members.

Buket had a difficult pregnancy, and although, as she put it, she was not religious, she prayed and promised that if the baby lived to be a year old, she would offer a religious sacrifice. A son was born; during the next sacrificial holiday (*Kurban Bayramı*), she wanted to sacrifice a sheep, but she said that it was unheard of for a woman to buy a sheep. Her husband was out of town, so her mother asked Buket's brother to buy it. When he brought the sheep, Buket asked him how much it had cost. He said curtly, "What's it to you?" She argued with him, saying that if it were just a pair of shoes, she wouldn't mention it, but that in order for it to be *her* sacrifice, she had to pay for it. Reluctantly, her brother agreed and told her the price.

Exchanging Debts

In Turkey it is precisely the putting off of the countergift (I include here labor and other services) which joins people and groups in elastic but durable relations that create both solidarity and dependence in social relationships ranging from those within the family to those in the marketplace. The countergift is delayed indefinitely or temporarily, depending on the relative personal/business content of the relation.

In a sense, it is less an exchange of gifts than an exchange of debts. Children are bonded to their mothers by an unrepayable "milk debt" (*süt hakkı*[3]), which is predicated in large part on the labor their mother has expended for them since their birth. In business transactions among friends, money debts are desirable (if temporary) markers of a personal indebtability derived from the reciprocal nature of the friendship.

While indebtedness is intrinsic to reciprocity and necessary for maintaining the open-endedness of social relations upon which social solidarity (and consequent security) rests, there is also a strong moral imperative to release the other person from reciprocal obligations. This is done in a ritual fashion in order to avoid the suspicion that favors have been done in order to get something in return—that is, to incur unlawful profit, profit which has been obtained through coercion.

The avoidance of apparent profit in personal relations is codified as a ritual verbal exchange between people who have been together, for example as friends or as business associates, and who are parting. Each person says to the other "Hakkın kaldıysa helâl et," which can be loosely translated as "If any unjust profit (from our relationship) remains with you, give up your lawful claim to it," or "If you retain any (reciprocal) moral debt (to me for things I have done for/given to you), let (the profit) be religiously lawful. I have given it to you with my heart and of my free will." The phrase "Hakkını helâl et" is difficult to translate exactly because the words that comprise it have multiple meanings: *hak* means right, justice, and law as well as share, due, remuneration, and fee; *helâl* means canonically lawful. When combined with the verb "to make" (*etmek*), it means to give up a legitimate claim to another and not to begrudge something done or given.

Reciprocal relations between people as well as business relations involving money and profit are understood, then, by reference to a religious ethic wherein profit is unlawful unless that which has profited the person was given freely and fairly. If person A has done more for person B than person B for person A, person B remains under a moral obligation (*manevi borç*, literally "moral debt") to person A. This means that person A has more *hak*, more right. Upon parting, such an imbalance must be corrected, according to Tibet, a middle-aged, educated civil servant, because otherwise person A has done more good (deeds) and could remind person B of them. This means that person A has not done these things from the heart but wanted something.

The ritual forgiving of moral debts does not imply a disapproval of indebtedness or a desire for closure in the relationship, but rather a fear, as Bourdieu would put it, of making conscious what must remain hidden (or misrecognized) in order that reciprocity continue to be seen as a social relation devoid of naked economic (unlawful, profit-oriented) motives.

This ritual abnegation of the profit motive points up the importance of maintaining the personal (and reciprocal) nature of all transactions, be they between friends or between business partners. Only among strangers is a market transaction allowed to be nakedly economic (and profit-oriented), featuring immediate payment for measured goods or services.[4] There is, after such a transaction, no further expectation, no debt, and no personal relation. Only after repeated transactions of this kind between the same people does a reciprocal relation begin to emerge, as the buyer has shown loyalty to the seller. After someone has established a pattern of patronizing the same shop, the buyer can expect to be extended credit, given a reduction in price, offered tea and conversation—all markers of a reciprocal relation. These can be seen as offers of indebtedness to create a personal/business bond.

As the history of reciprocity in the relationship accumulates, the business relation takes on elements of personal obligation (for example, to buy from a particular shop). The naked economic aspects of the relation (buying, selling, money, profit) become euphemized as personal relations of loyalty, trust, and membership in a group (or grouping, as between two people) as friends or symbolic kin.

Whether the relation is purely personal, as within a family, or relatively impersonal, as between almost strangers, the exchange of debts allows each person to partake in the solidarity, mutual dependency, and consequent survival of the group as a whole. Each person in Turkish society belongs to and is busily developing and strengthening membership in many such groups or groupings. As a consequence, outsiders find it frustrating to attempt even such relatively simple projects as having a telephone connected or picking up a parcel from the post office, because the outsider does not have access to the chain of people linked through reciprocal indebtedness that ordinarily provides access to these goods or services.

When two strangers in Turkey meet, often the first thing they do is to verbally sift through a list of people they might know in common. They are looking for a reciprocal link on which to base a personal relationship. Reciprocity, then, gives access to more than a particular group or grouping, but rather to a varied web of relations which are linked through reciprocal indebtedness, involving people whom the individual may not know directly. Before attempting any project or major purchase, a person sifts through all the connections at his or her disposal and sets in motion one or more relations (calling in a debt, so to speak, thereby creating a new debt) to activate the strands to which they are connected, with the ultimate purpose of getting as close as possible to the source of the desired service or product. To connect a telephone, the ideal contact is a friend or "friend of a friend" (*torpil*, "push," "influence") who works for the telephone company. The service is thereby made possible (at the time of my research, it could take up to six years to have a phone connected without a *torpil*), or the product acquired more cheaply.

The Power of Debt

Debt-exchange creates a web of relations in which every individual has access to different strands of debt-based relations. The strands available to an individual are constantly being added to and sometimes being blocked as new relations are formed and old ones cut. Like gifts exchanged, debts are created by individuals meeting face-to-face. Debt-exchange differs from gift-exchange, however, in that debts can be called in, through a reciprocal strand, from individuals that one has never met. Thus, to have a telephone installed, a person may activate a strand of many people that begins with a friend and ends with a complete stranger who is employed by the telephone company and who facilitates the installation.

Gift-exchange, while it may involve chains of people, as in Malinowski's description of the Trobriand Kula ring (1922), nevertheless ultimately takes place between two people, the gift-giver and the giver of the countergift, with the ball being, so to speak, in one court or the other. The gift is always followed by a countergift (Van Baal 1975:23). In debt-exchange, on the other hand, the ball is always in play: that is, while gifts must be returned, debts can be passed on. The individual's position in a family web and social web of reciprocal debt is continually shifting and being renegotiated. There is no closure, no final and direct return of a gift (except in an exchange of presents).

The currency of negotiation among women is primarily labor. Women's preparation of food for other women's weddings, engagements, birth celebrations, and other ceremonies, for example, is not so much a gift of food as a contribution which assures that those women are included in the web of mutual support. This network provides for the redistribution of such necessities of life as food, labor, and information, and the exchange of children in marriage. Food preparation is not a gift that must be reciprocated in kind at a later time, but one of many varied means of access to a web of indebtedness which underlies the process of survival.

Membership in relations of indebtedness involve one in relations of power and domination. Bourdieu writes that "giving is also a way of possessing (a gift which is not matched by a counter-gift creates a lasting bond. . . .)" (1979:195). He argues that this is a form of reconversion of economic capital into symbolic capital, a source of power.

> Agents lastingly "bind" each other, not only as parents and children, but also as creditor and debtor, master and *khammes*, only through the dispositions which the group inculcates in them and continuously reinforces, and which render *unthinkable* practices which would appear as legitimate and even be taken for granted in the disenchanted economy of "naked self-interest." (Ibid.: 195–196)

The notion of symbolic capital is a useful one for understanding reciprocal bonding, but it is based on direct relations between individuals (cf. ibid.:191). Gifts are met by countergifts of homage, respect, loyalty, work, and service (ibid.:195), thereby masking the dissymmetry of the relationship in a semblance of ordered closure. A system of debt-exchange, on the other hand, gives access to much greater symbolic (and material) treasure: it gives continual access without closure to the services and favors of countless known and unknown persons in all arenas of society. Furthermore, it is flexible, and the strand of relations can be selected according to need.

Also, while certain reciprocal ties euphemize relations of asymmetrical power, the balance may change according to which reciprocal strands are activated. An individual is less powerful than some in the family and social web but is simultaneously more powerful than others in the web. Domination through debt, then, also partakes of the complexity of construction of family and social relations and cannot profitably be seen only as a result of face-to-face dyadic relations. Such dyadic relations are important as the initiating interface of reciprocal strands in the social web and are the points at which power relations are practiced and negotiated.

If, as Bourdieu writes, giving is also a way of possessing, then it becomes clear that the close relation in Turkey between mother and son, for example, is based on a mother's labor and moral contribution to her son's welfare and on the son's inability to repay his debt to her. The son attempts to repay his debt, but as he is not able to do so, the debt he carries is converted to homage, respect, loyalty, and so on, the intangibles that make up the symbolic capital on which a mother bases her future well-being and which give her considerable power and authority over her son.

If, however, one takes another family relation, that of *gelin* and mother-in-law, this conversion does not occur. The *gelin*, as described in a previous chapter, gives a great deal of time, labor, service, and often material benefit to her mother-in-law. Nevertheless, this does not give the *gelin* power over the mother-in-law; quite the contrary. On the one hand, the *gelin* is in an inferior position to the mother-in-law in terms of social hierarchy. A gift of labor from an inferior to a superior would not incur debt but rather would be an expression of a patronage relationship.

On the other hand, I have argued in previous chapters that the *gelin* must be seen as embedded within a set of interrelated relationships rather than as an individual in a hierarchy. Her relationship with her mother-in-law can only be understood within the context of her husband's relationship with his mother.

The *gelin* is part of a triadic relationship including her husband and his mother, and her labor and services are an expression of the son's debt to his mother. The powerful relation of indebtedness between mother and son allows the mother to absorb the son's wife's labor and services as a part of her son's debt. In so doing, the mother-in-law does not allow the *gelin* the opportunity to transform her labor into debts (for *any* member of the husband's family, including his siblings), thereby depriving the *gelin* of the means to create solidarity with the husband's family and of the means to power within that context. The mother-in-law's authority over the *gelin* is predicated upon her participation in *her husband's* indebtedness.

The construction of unrepayable debts is a source of power and domination not only within the family but throughout Turkish society. Power may be transformed into authority, following Bourdieu, by euphemizing the aspects of self-interest in a relationship: construction of unrepayable debts into the moral authority of a mother over her children (through the accumulation of symbolic capital); denial of indebtedness into the moral authority of a mother-in-law over the *gelin*. Where there is extraction of labor and other services by moral force, there is only limited need for overt violence.

Power, in these cases, is not a male/female construction, nor is it related to public/private contexts. It is, rather, an individual mobilization and strategic manipulation of the reciprocal social web within which power is distributed. The mother-in-law's ability to deny indebtedness to the *gelin* cannot be seen in isolation from her other reciprocal relations. The power which the mother-in-law derives from the (unrepayable) debt-bonds with her son and other children, for example, translates into the authority by which she demands labor and services from her daughter-in-law.

As we have seen, public and private spheres do act in Turkey as strong ideological (and physical) constructs that reinforce gender and age role differences. All members of Turkish society, however, have access to some degree of power through the manipulation of reciprocal debts. Individuals are usually both dominated and dominant depending on their position in the strands of reciprocal relations that have been activated.

Relations of domination, then, in the sphere of economic behavior as well as within the family, are euphemized as relations of kinship or friendship. The coercive power of economic relations is misrecognized as reciprocal obligation, just as within the family labor exploitation is misrecognized as obligation inherent in the role identity of family members. In both cases, power and domination are played out simultaneously at multiple levels, whereby an individual can be both dominant and dominated at the same time.

Power is a process encoded in the shifting web of family and social relations. That is, power is created by all members of the society in practice through the manipulation of reciprocal debts but is at the same time limited in its potential practice by this very definition. Power can be practiced only within the parameters of a social web[5] from which there is no escape.[6]

I have suggested in this chapter that reciprocity and the exchange of debts (and attendant obligations) are a source of power and thus domination—and exploitation—throughout Turkish society. I have discussed this particularly with regard to the exploitation of labor within the family, where exploitation is euphemized as obligations embedded in role identity, and with regard to economic behavior in general, where business and the extraction of profit are euphemized as obligations inherent in kinship and friendship.

I have also argued that power is always in the process of being created, since it is the product of relations not only between individuals but also among the strands of the social web which contain them. Thus, as debts are called in (or accumulated), other debts are simultaneously created within the web. The social web at one and the same time offers power to all and restricts the practice of power to what can be accomplished within the web. People are dependent on one another both to dominate and to survive.

In the following chapters, I will describe how the family and the economic sector articulate in the construction of piecework, a system of labor exploitation which is based both on the assimilation of labor obligations to women's self-identity within the family and on the euphemization of business as kinship. Piecework and family labor each are a way in which the web of reciprocal obligations and relations of indebtedness provides support to individuals within groups and within society as a whole in what appear to be insupportable economic circumstances. The family and social web, then, is a source of power and constraint, domination and oppression, safety, limitation, and (contested) identity, and is the site where these contradictions are expressed in practice.

PART 3
THE STRUCTURE OF PRODUCTION

Leather garments on display at a merchant's shop. These are pieced together with simple crochet; others are more elaborate.

Piecework distributor in the storefront where he receives merchants who wish to place or pick up orders.

Wife of a piecework distributor standing in their workshop next to a portrait of Mustafa Kemal Atatürk.

Chapter 7
Money Makes Us Relatives

In this chapter I will discuss the organization of family labor in Istanbul, giving particular attention to the organization of piecework labor. I suggest here that in Istanbul small-scale commodity production is structured in a similar way whether it is individual production in the home (independently for friends or on an organized piecework basis), in a piecework atelier, or in a family atelier where production occurs entirely on the premises.

A corollary to my argument for the similarity of individual production, piecework production, piecework ateliers, and family ateliers is that spatial location—that is, whether production occurs within the household or in a separate location—is not a necessary defining characteristic of this type of production.

The similarity of these forms of production is grounded in their basic premise of production for pay in response to product orders taken from outside the household, atelier, or community. In addition, all use family labor. The labor of women and children is associated with their identity as group members and is consequently devalued as a resource. The labor relations themselves generally are euphemized as (actual or fictive) kinship.

The results of this research support Friedmann's (1986) suggestion that the deployment of resources within small-scale commodity production under capitalism is governed by a kinship logic. I would add that in the Istanbul squatter districts this kinship logic extends to persons who are not kin but who are in a reciprocal relationship with one another, regardless of whether this relationship involves services, labor, or money (as in the exchange of labor for money in piecework production).

Related to this "kinship rationality" is an avoidance of risk taking and an attitude toward growth and reinvestment that emphasizes social status and immediate benefit over long-term strategy and growth. Finally, all these levels of organization of production have links to the world market.[1] Risk taking and attitudes toward investment and growth will be discussed in the following chapter.

Role of the Household

While most authors concerned with small-scale commodity production under capitalism agree that use of family labor is a basic characteristic, they do not agree on whether or not and in what capacity the household is a constituent part of small-scale production. Although small-scale production in Istanbul involves family labor, it does not require the household, as it has generally been defined as a physical or coresidential unit,[2] either as a site of production or as a site for the organization of production. The site for a family atelier can vary over time from within the household to separate premises, with spatial gradations in between. Similarly, a single site of production can move fluidly from one form of organization to another. This will be illustrated in Chapter 8 by an account of the life cycle of a single atelier.

While women's production often takes place within the household, this is not a necessary criterion. The social content of the relations of production rather than any spatial preference constitute women's particular access to this type of production. Thus women can work anywhere in the neighborhood or even in a different neighborhood among friends and relatives without substantially affecting the social definition of their labor as "not work." In other words, the relations of production of a woman working at home doing piecework and a woman working in an atelier away from her home are both primarily determined by their membership in social groups as family, kin, and neighbor, rather than by such considerations as the location of their productive efforts.

Another traditional criterion for determining the relations of production of a particular labor activity is whether or not the producing individuals control their means of production and their labor. In the Turkish case, relations of production are often (although not exclusively) determined by the usufruct rights conferred onto group members over the labor of other members and over the means of production. Just as women's labor power can be the property of the group rather than the individual, so can the means of production in the atelier be considered the property of the family. This constitutes a type of economic ownership different from legal ownership in that family membership confers usufruct rights over the means of production as well as over the labor of each member.

Thus, relations of production can be defined in the Istanbul case as constituted by economic ownership (that is, ownership in practice) of productive forces by the group in the name of, rather than instead of, the individual. Furthermore, group relations which are at the base of these relations of production are not necessarily coterminous with individual family relations. Rethinking these relations poses a difficulty in defining the site of production as the household and producers as family labor.

Friedman suggests an alternative definition of household "not as a determinate set of people but as a set of relationships that impose a mutual obligation to pool resources from a multiplicity of labor forms whether or not one of those resources is a common residence" (1984:48). Redefined in this way as sets of relations between people that impose sharing obligations, households take on broader boundaries. Nevertheless, even in its broader manifestation as an income-pooling unit, the household is limited by other internal structures of allocation of tasks and rewards. It would be difficult to include neighbors and nonkin in any kind of definition of small-scale production that involved the household, no matter how broad the definition.

Income pooling and the reciprocity and obligation that it implies, however, do bind groups, although they may be neither related nor live together. As we have seen, income pooling is a common practice in Istanbul even among members of groups that do not constitute a household, such as women's social groups or groups of co-workers.

Relations of production in Turkish small-scale production consist of sets of relations among family, kin, fictive kin, and neighbors, without the necessity of coresidentiality. Much production occurs within the household or is organized from within the household, and family members contribute a great deal of the labor involved in production. Nevertheless, the household or actual kinship are not necessary factors in defining small-scale production. It can, however, be defined as a set of individual relations of production constituted by group economic ownership of individual labor and the means of production. Such labor relations transcend household and kinship boundaries, although they need not do so.

In the following sections, I will describe in detail the various types of organization of family labor found in Istanbul. It will be clear from these examples that while the form of production may or may not be coterminous with a household (using either definition), the relations of production are constructed in the same way regardless of the particular level of organizational complexity or location of production. The labor of individuals is subsumed by relations of production predicated upon group ownership of that labor and group control of the means of production.

That these relations (the group in the name of the individual) mask economic exploitation will also be made clear. At its most basic, exploitation means "value appropriated from someone who produced it by someone who did not" (Durrenberger 1980: 139). The surplus value produced by the individual labor of these women is appropriated by the group as a whole and by the intermediary in particular, but also by the merchants who resell their products locally and on the world market.

Organization of Labor

Family labor in Istanbul is organized in a number of different ways. Small-scale production using family labor in its least complex manifestation can mean simply an individual producing articles in the home that have been requested by and are sold to friends and neighbors. An individual (male or female) works at home, knitting, sewing, stitching, filling car batteries, doing repairs, woodwork, and so on, for neighbors or for friends.

Or individual production can be at the behest of a neighboring family filling orders for articles requested by a merchant from outside the neighborhood. The transition to piecework production is quite fluid, since the intermediary is often a relative or a neighbor, who acts as a central conduit for materials and orders obtained from outside the neighborhood, and for collecting and delivering the completed products and obtaining payment for them. Some of this money is then distributed among the neighbors at a set rate per piece produced. The rest is retained by the family of the distributor and generally is used to buy status items such as a VCR or car or to add another story to the family house.

This family might coordinate the production and sale of these articles from their home or might operate out of a small workshop. In some cases the workshop is a room set aside within the home or a room built onto the house especially for this purpose.

Production in many other ateliers[3] is not based on piecework but takes place entirely on the workshop premises, using family labor, apprentices, and salaried assistants. Such ateliers generally are situated on premises away from the home, are registered as small businesses, and pay taxes. This particular form of organization of small production therefore has been more accessible to researchers and government enumerators. (See, for example, Çinar, Evcimen, and Kaytaz 1988; UNIDO 1987; Ayata 1982; and numerous publications by the Turkish State Planning Organization.)

In piecework production, however, the boundary between officially recognized business activity and individual economic action is more fluid. This ambiguity is reflected in the spatial organization of this type of production, which can take place in the home or in a separate workshop or in any spatial gradation in between. As we shall see in the example given in the next chapter of the development of a piecework atelier, a single family's production efforts may run the gamut both in terms of organizational complexity and in terms of spatial variation within the period of a single year.

Both piecework and the family atelier are particularly suited for the organization of women's labor in the squatter districts, since the women are able to reconcile earning additional income with traditional role constraints that discourage women from leaving the home, making contact with strangers, and taking over the male role of provider.

The more basic form of individual home production, where a woman produces items which she then "gives out" (sells) to other women, differs from women's piecework production primarily in terms of complexity. In both cases, the women receive orders for particular items from outside the home. The product is "given out" in exchange for money.

For individual producers as well as piecework and family ateliers, financial risk is avoided through a number of strategies; the person who orders the item also supplies the materials or prepays part of the cost so that materials can be purchased. Alternately, the producer or piecework distributor may lay in a stock of materials. However, only those materials that are certain to be used (for example white wool) are bought in any quantity. Other materials that reflect the requirements of a particular order (for example wool of a certain color) are purchased in quantities sufficient to meet that order. Production is expanded only in response to larger orders.

In addition to structure and avoidance of risk, individual home production, piecework production, and family atelier production have in common the ideological construction of women's labor as an expresssion of their social and gender identity and the euphemization of labor relations as social relations modeled (either actually or fictively) on family relations.

Individual Production

This section will describe production in the home at its least organized level, with individuals making products for friends, neighbors, relatives, and occasionally for people outside their close circle who are referred to them, such as the local schoolteacher. For women, this type of activity generally consists of sewing, knitting, or embroidery. Two women might work together, with one in effect subcontracting to the other.

The examples given below are taken from Ümraniye, a district on the Asian side of Istanbul. At its center, it is a teeming municipality of small shops and low-rise working-class apartment buildings, but at its edge Ümraniye's streets branch into a haphazard network of dirt roads threading together houses in various stages of completion. In many ways, Ümraniye is typical of Istanbul, with a largely migrant population and rapid, uncontrolled growth encroaching on the green hills of the city. Ümraniye was a squatter settlement during the city's rapid expansion after the 1950's, burgeoning with migrants from the disadvantaged rural areas. More recently, it has been incorporated into the city proper but, like Istanbul itself, remains a mixture of planned and unplanned housing, and a haven for newly arriving families. These families form a pool of largely unskilled[4] labor that has been tapped by industry and export entrepreneurs through a system of piecework (or putting out) and by subcontracting to ateliers that use family labor.

Hayriye

Hayriye, a woman who is skilled at the embroidery for which her Black Sea village is famous, embroiders nightgowns, blouses, headscarves, and doilies for neighbors and friends in Ümraniye. The nightgowns and matching dressing gowns are much sought after as trousseau items. Hayriye also occasionally knits sweaters for a merchant and is paid by the piece.

Her husband is a retired city bus driver, and the couple finds it difficult to live on his pension, particularly since the landlord, through machinations that bypassed rent-control laws, has recently raised their rent. Their two sons jointly own a taxi financed with their father's help. The married son drives it during the day and the unmarried son at night.

When Hayriye receives an order, she gives cloth to a neighbor woman (from the same Black Sea coast village) to sew the gowns which she then embroiders. She gives "special work," such as a blouse for her as yet unmarried son's future bride's trousseau, to her sister-in-law's daughter to sew.

Hayriye has a friend who also does such work on her own, and when there is a big order, they help each other. Recently, for example, the daughter of a distant relative wanted to take some embroidered items to the bank where she worked. She sold all of them in the minibus that took the workers to the bank in the morning, and asked Hayriye to make more.

Once or twice a year when she visits her village, Hayriye buys large bolts of the special *şile* cloth she needs for her gowns. She sends her husband or goes with him downtown to buy the embroidery thread in the colors and quantities she needs for a particular order. The neighbor woman owns her own sewing machine, but Hayriye provides all the other materials that the seamstress needs.

At present Hayriye has orders for six gown sets. "I can make two sets a month, if necessary faster." A nightgown yoke takes one and a half days to embroider, "including evenings, if I work straight through." The embroidery around the edges takes an additional day. The entire process, including cutting the cloth, takes three days. She can make three or four nightgowns (without dressing gowns; these take a great deal more embroidery) a week if she works almost continuously.

She charges 13,000 TL for a nightgown and 40,000 TL for a complete set. The cost of the cloth in a set is 20,000 TL. This leaves her with an income of 20,000 TL (about $22 [5]), minus the cost of thread and payment for sewing, for what I estimate to be about nine days' intensive labor cutting and embroidering a nightgown and dressing gown.

"At holidays work piles up so I do the urgent ones first. I am a housewife," she emphasizes, "and how much I can stitch depends on the time I have left over from housework and my other duties." Later she is careful to point out that she has also done this kind of labor for friends, neighbors, and relatives without expectation of payment. "In the past," she says, "I also knitted. I did this for whoever wanted a sweater and I didn't take money for it. I also did lacework, but not for myself; sometimes for neighbors. Although I didn't sell them. The others brought me the string."

Şengül

Şengül, also a resident of Ümraniye, machine-knits clothing for her friends. She is a Koran teacher who lives with her husband and two children in a four-story concrete apartment building on the outskirts of the neighborhood. She owns a knitting machine and produces clothing to sell to friends and neighbors. She is a plump, breathless woman with apple cheeks, dressed in a simple skirt and sweater, with a white cotton headscarf tied loosely at the nape of her neck. The knitting machine is set up in a room off the entrance hall. This room is also used to watch television, and for prayer. The knitting machine, looking like an electric organ, is set up by the window, positioned so that Şengül can work, watch her three young children, and talk to visitors while she is working.

Both Şengül and her husband are teachers in the local Koran school, but while her husband receives a small salary of 70,000 TL[6] a month, she receives only gratuities from her pupils' parents. By selling some land in the village, the couple had been able to buy a cooperative apartment when they first moved to Istanbul and were now spared rent payments, but they still had to pay their share of coal for heating, and other bills.

Şengül began machine-knitting two and a half years ago, she told me, bringing out for display a pile of clothing she had made for her own children. The variety of designs and the quality of the knitting were impressive. "I got the machine through my father's connections with a middleman who sold these machines and was going out of business. I bought it at the time for 375,000 TL,[7] and now such machines cost over a million liras. I paid off the machine completely and now I buy bread and milk from the proceeds." She taught herself to use the machine by trial and error, doing nothing else for two months, and complained that the instruction booklets were in a foreign language.

Şengül buys large quantities of yarn at a time on credit. She said she has paid off 250,000 TL worth of yarn. She doesn't buy it regularly, just when she needs it, and then she buys it wholesale from a downtown merchant. At the same time, she also buys thread for the crocheted edgings and stitched designs she adds to little table mats that she knits on the machine. She either does the edgings herself or has them done for her. "In the winter, I make pullovers, vests, and sweaters; I made a dress for the local teacher, and children's clothes."

Whenever the conversation skirted close to questions about why she was doing this knitting, Şengül would become sweaty and fidgety and begin to explain: "I really don't do a lot of this. Just once in a while." "I don't sell it outside. My friends come and want something and I make it for them." It was clear that she was puzzled by my interest in her activities, since I had been introduced to her as someone interested in women "working" at home (*evde çalışan ka-*

dınlar), and she did not see herself as belonging to a category of people who do regular work, sell their product to strangers, and rely on the money earned in this way. "I never take orders from a merchant," she insisted. "I use my own model and my own yarn. Or the yarn of the woman who wants the sweater."

When I asked Şengül when she does the knitting and how long it takes her to finish one sweater, she answered, "I don't do a lot of it. I have housework, I watch the children, and I sit." She indicated the assembled company of neighborhood women who had joined her for tea. "I don't have time," she continued. "The women bring the things they want and they come themselves to get them." Later, she admitted that she could make a sweater in one day if she worked continuously, but that she usually took two days to make one.

She added that she knew another woman who did this continuously, but that her daughter was grown up (implying that she had no child care duties). Another woman chimed in saying, "But she only makes placemats." Everyone began to speak at once: "She doesn't know [how to use the machine]. She makes them plain, without decoration, and sells them to a merchant." "She works like a bold busybody!" "She puts them in a bag and takes them to sell to the merchants." "She's very shrewd, very different. She knows her work, that one!" "The woman leaves them at the stores. She knows how to profit from things!" "You should see how she knows this area." They were scornful of her "knowing" the neighborhood, being out on the street where she had no business being, talking to strange men, and of her interest in profit.

By their own definition "good" Muslim wives do not work outside the home among strangers, and those that do are morally suspect and subject to ridicule. Under the present difficult economic circumstances,[8] however, additional income often is needed for a family to survive. While many men also work at more than one job, women and children are able to contribute to the family's economic security in two ways—directly through income derived from their labor, and indirectly by reaffirming their membership in the community through the contribution and exchange of labor. As long as individual production, piecework, and atelier labor are seen to be an expression of group identity and solidarity, rather than "work," they remain morally and socially acceptable. Through the contribution and exchange of labor—paid and unpaid—women like Şengül participate in the reciprocal obligation and redistribution that characterize these groups and that provide the foundation for group security.

As I argued in the preceding chapters, however, the association of labor with women's (and children's) role identity allows their labor to be poorly remunerated if at all. Since the women insist that this labor is not work, they neither keep track of time spent working nor figure hourly rates for their labor. When Şengül was asked how many sweaters she made a month, she said she had no idea. "Not really that many. Last month," she said slowly, deliberating, "I had guests from the village so I couldn't do very many. About fifteen I guess. I have some time in the evening, between nine and ten, when I can work. I also have to sew the parts together." At this, a murmur went around the room among the other women, "You make a *lot!*" Since Şengül had estimated that it takes her two days to make a sweater, fifteen sweaters a month meant that she worked every day. Şengül looked embarrassed and I quickly changed the subject.

The Piecework Atelier

In most working-class neighborhoods, individual women's labor also is mobilized around a steady source of demand for that labor—ateliers run by families that give out piecework to the women in the neighborhood. As in individual production, the ateliers allow the women to maintain the connection between their labor and their identity. Thus while a woman is working at home, producing for pay a product destined for the local or world market, she is encouraged to see that labor as part of her role as woman, as family member, and as neighbor.

She is encouraged to do so both by the attitudes of the other women and by her employers, all of whom entwine the woman's labor with the other social activities that bind them together. Thus a woman knitting a piecework sweater generally will do this in the company of other women, or even in the home of the woman who is organizing the piecework. In one newly built squatter settlement along the main Istanbul-Ankara highway, it is not uncommon in the middle of the afternoon to see large knots of women standing in the dirt lanes chatting, each one knitting,[9] generally sweaters for the intermediary who has set up a piecework operation there.

The labor relation is euphemized as a social bond. This is most clear in the relation between family members who contribute unpaid labor to their family atelier. A family atelier may or may not send out materials to be made up as piecework. While my research encompassed ateliers that employed family members and manufactured articles entirely on the premises, I will concentrate here on the organization of ateliers that are constructed primarily around piecework.

In both cases, the relation of labor to identity is maintained and work is seen to be an expression of the individual's role as group member. While this seems clear in the case of unsalaried family labor, it is perhaps more difficult to demonstrate with the labor of unrelated women who are given piecework by a neighborhood family.

For this reason, following a more general description of piecework production, I will give a detailed account of one such atelier in a squatter settlement on the European shore of the Bosphorus. This account will show how the atelier is structured as a business. That is, it will clearly reveal the business nature of the labor relations in the piecework process and their connection to the world market. This example will also demonstrate the metaphors by which these relations are euphemized as personal relations, indeed as relations of fictive kinship.

In General

Piecework can be done on an individual basis for friends and neighbors, or can be more structured, with whole neighborhoods working for a particular intermediary, making products that are often exported. It is practiced mainly by women and children and involves items that can be produced or finished by hand. Women's participation in wage labor outside the home in Istanbul squatter areas was estimated to be as low as 5.5 percent in 1976 (Şenyapılı 1981). In 1988 only 16.9 percent of all urban women in Turkey were employed.[10]

Distribution usually takes place in cooperation with other family members and is organized by gender. The person dealing with the world outside of the neighborhood is usually a father, brother, or other male relative. He obtains the orders and materials and brings them into the neighborhood. His wife distributes the materials to their female neighbors and collects the finished pieces. As one piecework distributor explained, the women do the homework and the men do the selling because "the ladies' contacts are there, and the men's in the market."

The husband keeps the books and pays out the money to the women for their work. This is usually done once or twice a month. However, the women are paid only after the distributor receives the money for the finished products. If there is a delay, the women must wait, sometimes for months, for payment.

Payment for one or more pieces is always withheld to ensure that the women will return with the materials they were given to work with in the next batch. This also has the effect of inducing loyalty, since the women must always return and, when there, generally ask for another batch of work, rather than for final payment. Once final payment is made, the "books are closed" on a woman's name, and she may have difficulty returning to work for this distributor in the future.

A room may be set aside in the home and become a small work-shop where materials are prepared, stored, distributed, and collected. If production expands, a small storefront may be rented nearby, and young neighborhood girls and boys hired to supplement the labor of the family members in preparing materials to be distributed. Scraps of leather, for example, must be cut into long strips so that they can be knitted into vests, or cut into shapes and hole-punched along their edges so that they can be crocheted together and joined into skirts and tops destined for export to Europe.

In Particular: Yenikent

The squatter district of Yenikent is situated on a bare hill overlooking the Bosphorus, up a steep hill from a relatively affluent neighborhood along the shore. The neighborhood is a welter of cement block houses in various stages of completion. There is one main road, unpaved, leading down the hill through areas of open land to the older neighborhood by the shore.

Going in the other direction, this same road emerges through stands of pine and joins a main thoroughfare that skirts the western part of the city. The infrequent city bus from central Istanbul travels along this road for nearly an hour before turning off to make its final stop in front of the mosque in Yenikent, where it turns around and returns to the city center.

The ground floors of some of the buildings along the central road have been fitted with plate-glass windows and turned into shops selling appliances, furniture, and clothing. A fairly large new mosque dominates the road. There are no other streets, only muddy lanes, but the houses seem sturdy, built of cement block. Some are two- and three-story apartment dwellings. They are built helter-skelter, with the configuration of lanes emerging as an afterthought to the construction of houses and gardens. Some houses had only recently been torn down by the municipality because they had been constructed without permission.

My guide is Serap, a maid, who is taking me to visit her maternal uncle's daughter-in-law. Serap leads me toward a tiny cement block house, no more than a small room, faced by a door and a large pane of glass through which I can see fruits and vegetables displayed for sale. The vegetable shop is also owned by a relative, she explains. The concrete shack is built onto the front of a slightly larger structure, also of unplastered cement blocks.

Serap guides me down the steep muddy alley between this house and a neighboring one. At the end of the alley we turn and enter another cement structure, essentially a twenty-foot-square room attached to the bottom of the incline below the vegetable shop.

The room is divided in the middle by a wooden barrier. Beyond it I can see shelves of supplies, yarn, leather scraps in little bundles, and an old manual fruit vendor's scale on a table. On the side by the entrance there are a coal stove, a desk, a padded bench, and a few chairs. On the wall hang framed portraits of Kemal Atatürk and Adnan Menderes,[11] as well as a large poster of Turgut Özal, then prime minister, a map of Turkey, and a framed verse from the Koran. On the opposite wall is a calendar drawing of a large-eyed sad little boy.

I am introduced to Hatice and her husband Osman, owners of the atelier. Hatice is thirty-one. Her face is round and healthy looking with even, pretty features. She is quick to smile. Osman is a slim man with dark brown hair and a mustache, in his midthirties. They have four children. The eldest, Emine, is a fifteen-year-old girl, the youngest a seven-year-old boy. He is the only son and is named Uğur, which means "good luck." Four photographs of Uğur adorn the office wall. There are no photographs of the girls. Emine is pretty, round-faced, fresh-cheeked, with a shy smile. Her two younger sisters are still thin and awkward, dressed in cheap cotton dresses and sweaters.

They live in a rented apartment on the second floor of an unplastered cement block house one hundred yards down a muddy slope from the workshop. To enter the apartment, they must first climb a makeshift rickety wooden ladder. Beyond the entrance hall, where one leaves one's shoes, is a long narrow room with a *somya* (a large bed with cushions, also used for sitting) across the back, a narrow upholstered bench along the side, and a glowing coal stove in the front.

There are doors leading off each side of the room, closed in winter to contain the heat of the stove. On one side is a kitchen and a bedroom, on the other a seldom used parlor and, a little way down the hall, a bathroom. The furniture is sparse and shabby. In the parlor is a machine-made rug.

The Products. The atelier produces vests made of leather strips knitted together, and matching tops and skirts made of large diamond-shaped patches of very fine leather attached by means of crocheted panels of shiny yarn (*floş*). The tops can also be made of smaller or irregularly shaped pieces of leather and sold separately as T-shirts. Very rarely the atelier takes an order for knitted sweaters. Almost all of the products of the atelier are exported or sold to merchants catering to tourists. "Our product isn't local," Osman says. "No one wears it here, only in Europe. It's also too expensive for local people."

Hatice took the idea for the two-piece outfit from a European magazine, only raising the neckline somewhat. She and her family make up samples, and Osman brings them to shops and merchants or intermediaries to see if they would like to place an order for such pieces. Alternatively, a merchant may bring in an exemplar and place an order. If the merchant has not provided his own materials, Osman finds the materials himself and buys them with money given to him in advance for this purpose.

Osman says that in the past the leather used to be very poor quality ("*terlik*" houseshoe leather) and smelled terrible, but that now they can get very fine leather scraps, some of which come from ateliers in France. Balls of scrap leather from ateliers in France are bought by Şişli[12] leather ateliers which use the larger sheets of leather themselves and sell the smaller scraps for about 3,000 TL per kilo (depending on the quality).

Family members, with the assistance of a young neighborhood girl, prepare the leather, cutting it into shape and making the holes to attach the yarn. The family then gives the materials to neighborhood women and tells them what to do. The women come into the workshop to look at the model. For the knitted leather vests, the women take the leather scraps home and cut them into strips there.

The Producers. Osman has a book that lists the women doing piecework. Each woman has a page on which is noted what she took and what she brought back. The women, he explains, are mostly married women, although there are a few young girls. Emine's friend Güllü adds, "Young girls don't have time because they are making their trousseaux."

Osman says he had up to forty women working for him a month ago. "I dropped the number to thirty because I couldn't give them all work all the time. I dropped the ones whose work wasn't so good. Now I have ten occasional and thirty regular women."

Of the women who come to take away piecework, Osman says, "some of the women do a lot, some a little. Some lazy women only do two a month. One industrious woman did four skirts and sixteen tops last month." If one calculates five hours labor per piece, this means that the woman worked two hundred hours that month, more than forty hours a week! For this she earned 42,000 TL ($47). The minimum wage at this time (April 1987) was 41,400 TL ($46[13]) but was raised only two months later to 74,250 TL ($82.50) (Çinar 1989:19). Osman, however, did not increase the amount he paid for the women's labor. Indeed, the piece-rate was raised only minimally during the entire year.[14]

"This woman," Osman goes on, "is middle-aged, married, and has one child who goes to school." The implication is that she has a great deal of free time. "Another woman," he explains, "who did fifteen tops and two skirts, has two grown daughters who help her with the housework and free her for this work." Judging from my observations of women doing piecework in their homes, it is probable that this woman's daughters and perhaps daughters-in-law do some of the crochet as well.

Hatice sees all the women who work for them socially "because they are neighbors." "They meet now and then for afternoon gatherings for tea and conversation at different people's homes. They tell one another which house it's at." Hatice says she herself doesn't work in the atelier very much anymore or knit because she has a lot of housework now. She does, however, knit samples and models. Later she shows me a child's sweater of pink and blue wool with embroidered wool flowers, which she says Osman had brought home from a dealer to see if she could copy it.

Workers as Kin.   The women who do the work generally are neighbors, although some women come from other nearby neighborhoods. Anyone is free to come in and look at the exemplars to see if they can do the work, explains Hatice. Murad, a neighbor who runs his own piecework atelier, adds, "They are stranger women [*yabancı kadın*], but they are *para ile akraba olanları* [ones who have been made kin through money]."

When I ask Osman what this means, he explains, "If you give (them) money, they do it." When I look puzzled, he adds, "If you give money to someone, they become kin." He continues, "In Anatolia there is something called *imece çalışma*,[15] or *bedelsiz*.[16] Or you can also say *ırgat*.[17] You do something for me; I do something for you with no expectation of return. For example, in the villages they do this with gathering fruit, sowing, and harvesting so that the things won't dry up. For example, Güllü[18] punches holes in two of these outfits a day and then takes them home, without pay." I ask why. "Because she likes us." I ask if he is joking with me. "No joke," he insists. Emine tries to clarify things by stating, "She's my best friend." Güllü, looking serious, adds, "We're sisters." I sense a general feeling of consternation about why I don't believe or don't understand the situation.

In their explanation above, Osman, Murad, and the others do not differentiate between donated labor such as Güllü's and paid labor such as that of the women who came from another neighborhood to get piecework. In their view, the women are kin (*akraba*) by virtue of their participation in the exchange of labor for money, providing of course that this is done in the spirit of *imece*—that is, as collective reciprocal assistance with no expectation of return. Although the relation between Osman and the women from another neighborhood, at least, is based on a commercial transaction (payment for labor), it is euphemized here as a kin relation (involving open-ended reciprocity). Güllü's donation of labor without pay to the workshop also is explained in kinship terms; she is Emine's "sister."

Kinship is metaphorically conferred, then, on those people who participate in relations of collective reciprocal assistance with no expectation of return. These relations may or may not involve payment for labor, but the payment of money for labor has the same role as an exchange of labor or services in terms of participation in a reciprocal relationship. Indeed, money *makes* them relatives. In other words, these fictive kin relations are constructed in the same way as actual kin relations, which, as I have argued in a previous chapter, are also based on participation in a web of reciprocal obligation and indebtedness.

Money as kin-maker is patently a myth, since the women generally do expect to receive money for the sweaters they knit. However, money in this situation has become a thing or a service, emptied of its capitalist and market content. Money is a thing which can be freely given, just as labor (within this mythic refraction of meaning) is freely given. Even when money is given as money—that is, expressing a market value—loans and debts among kin are not openly expected to be repaid. Repayment need not necessarily be in the form of money; certainly it should not be immediate.

It is Osman, the piecework atelier owner, who insisted on the mystical power of money to make strangers kin, that is, to bind them to him in relations of open-ended reciprocal exchange of labor for money, of thing for thing, service for service. I do not know whether or not the "stranger women" from another neighborhood also thought this way about their relation with Osman. I would doubt this, judging from the attitudes of women in another squatter area who work for a distributor who is not a member of the community. The "stranger distributor" perceived the women who worked for him paternalistically as children for whom he was responsible. The women, however, saw him as a source of money for labor and did not express any kinship-related attitudes toward him.

The expectation of a kin-type relation—that is, one of reciprocal obligation—seems to be an intrinsic part of the distributor's relation to the women who work for him, since it provides the ideological foundation for the organization of (and rate of payment for) the women's labor. However, it is not necessarily reciprocated. Women or girls from the community do not donate labor without pay to the atelier of the stranger distributor, nor would the stranger women donate their labor to Osman's atelier.

However, in those piecework ateliers where the distributor and the women who do the piecework are neighbors, the relation of labor for money on both sides is overlaid with feelings of group solidarity. Labor, whether paid or unpaid, is seen as part of the obligation for mutual assistance that is required for group membership.

The Turkish word for kin, *akraba*, originates in Arabic, and its etymology provides a broader set of meanings within which proximity, relationship, and kinship are given equal place. *Akraba*, which means "kin" or "relative" in Turkish, is derived from the Arabic root *qaruba*, meaning "to be near." Another form of the same Arabic root is *qurba*, meaning "relation, relationship, or kinship." Yet another form of the root is *aqrab*, meaning "near, nearest." The plural of this can be *aqarib* or *aqrabun*, both of which mean "relations, relatives."

When business is slow, Osman says he employs only women from his own neighborhood and not from any other neighborhood. He does this because he feels he should employ neighbors first. "First those close to you, close neighbors." Then, if there is more work left, he employs women from other neighborhoods. He says this is because "you know your own neighbors and they're close by to pick up and deliver." I ask whether he feels an obligation toward his neighbors because they are neighbors and whether it is shameful (*ayıp*) to leave neighbors without work. "Yes," he agrees, "it is *ayıp*."

Spending the Earnings.   The women work, Hatice says, because they need money. She explains that "if the husband's salary is too low, for example if he is a worker in a factory or in construction and gets 80,000–90,000 TL a month, the women work more then. The women working for us have husbands who make anywhere between 80,000–150,000 TL [$54–$60] or 200,000 TL [$134]." Sometimes children work "to pay for amusements" or to contribute to the household.

The women do the work, she says, in the empty hours after their housework is finished, while sitting with their husbands at night. They are paid once a month or every fifteen days and spend the money on things like clothing and children's needs. In answer to my question, she says some women give the money to their husbands if it is needed. "But the women's money is more for themselves and for the children and food."

The unmarried teenage girls either give the money to their mothers or use it to purchase materials for their trousseaux. Hatice illustrates, "Güllü gets 10,000 TL [$7] a week for five and a half days a week, about eight hours a day. She gives the money to her mother. Emine gets no salary."

Serap is a shy, short, fragile-looking girl with brown eyes and a large nose. She enters the workshop so quietly I don't hear her come in. She comes over and sits down to watch me experiment with T-shirt designs out of paper diamond shapes. She is dressed in an orange patterned skirt and long-sleeved yellow blouse, her head covered with a cotton scarf. I ask her if she works here. She responds that she and her mother earned 90,000 TL [$61] last month and 50,000 TL [$34] this month. I ask her if she doesn't need time to prepare her trousseau. Serap answers, "We're having it made." She explains that she has a liver disease and can't be vexed, so she can't make it herself. She and her mother use the money to have the trousseau made.

The women's income is used in traditionally female ways, for example to complete the inventory of such household items as pots and pans, carpets, and certain furniture that are traditionally the responsibility of the woman's side of the family at marriage and which they were perhaps too poor to afford at the time.

The women also use their earnings to purchase food and clothing for their children and perhaps to pay for school supplies. The women feel that they are primarily responsible for their young children, for their health, upbringing, and education. They say that their husbands take little consistent part in this, although they may make any final decisions, for example with regard to taking a daughter out of school.

Likewise, the income earned by the atelier generally is used by the distributor to improve the status of his family through purchase of large consumer items such as a VCR, a car, or better housing, all of which traditionally are the responsibility of the husband. The atelier's income may also be saved to expand the premises or change the location of the workshop. This is often related to an improvement in housing for the family (see Chapter 8).

The women may derive their income from, among other activities, individual production or piecework or, more rarely, from acting themselves as intermediaries between pieceworkers and merchants. Some of these merchants are also women. This makes it more socially acceptable for a squatter district woman to be an intermediary for pieceworkers in her neighborhood.

The female merchants work either on their own from their homes (and could more properly be called entrepreneurs) or together with an established company, usually an export firm. The women who work from their homes tend to be middle-class housewives with one or more contacts in the squatter districts.

Through the intermediary, these middle-class women place orders for knitted sweaters and crocheted, beaded, or embroidered items; they provide the models (sometimes just a page from a fashion magazine) and materials, and payment is made, also through the intermediary, after the finished products are received. The woman then sells these items to boutiques and individuals. It is quite likely that others of her female friends in the middle and upper middle classes own boutiques, as this is an occupation seen to be acceptable for women of that class to engage in.

In the case of one large export firm that distributes piecework for knitted sweaters to between five hundred and one thousand women in different areas of Istanbul, the company's representative to the squatter district women is a well-educated career woman named Aydan. A woman is elected by groups of pieceworkers as their intermediary with the company. Aydan explains that the woman chosen generally is physically strong and "a bit formidable" because she must get on a crowded city bus with thirty finished sweaters to bring them to the firm. "For example, if they don't let her on the bus and the driver says 'How can I take you with so much stuff?' they need a woman who can argue and take care of situations like that." The company offices are located in Nişantaşı, a crowded downtown business district. The "group chief" is also chosen for her knitting skills, since she knits the models and is in charge of quality control.

The "group chief" is paid a premium per number of sweaters completed and is also in charge of distributing an "incentive premium" after a shipment has been exported of 10 percent of the piecework wages. This is meant to encourage the women to produce more, since the more they knit, the higher the "incentive premium." In practice, however, the group head often keeps some of the money, saying she needs it to pay for transportation to the women's homes and to the firm. This situation gives her great status and influence among the other women who are dependent on her goodwill for payment. It is in the group head's interest, however, to maintain a cadre of satisfied good workers because her own payment is dependent upon their production.

Materials.   In his atelier in Yenikent, Osman buys the yarn for his leather outfits directly from the factory in Bursa, a city two hours by car from Istanbul. The type and amount of yarn he purchases is directly related to the orders he has. He would rather make the trip often, he says, than buy a lot of thread at once that he may then be unable to use. Indeed the shelves in the workshop where he stores excess materials are quite bare.

He buys the leather from various leather ateliers. Depending on the type of leather needed for a particular order, he goes from place to place until he finds what he wants. This cautious attitude toward purchasing supplies extends even to smaller items used in the workshop. For example, powder is sprinkled under the pieces of leather on the hole-punching machine so that they move more freely. This powder is bought one small envelope at a time and transferred to an empty round plastic La Vache Qui Rit container for use.

The leather outfits are made in three sizes, and any leftover pieces of leather from the smaller sizes are reused in other outfits. There is absolutely no waste. When Osman receives precut diamond-shaped pieces of leather from a merchant to be stitched together, these are packaged between pieces of cardboard of the same shape. Even these cardboard pieces are reused to measure leather cut in the workshop and to make cardboard models of new designs.

Production.   In the atelier, Osman takes orders over the phone, with occasional assistance by an unpaid male neighbor. Along with his daughter, and helped by her girlfriend, Osman cuts leather shapes for the tops and skirts and punches holes along their edges to which the crochet-work will be attached. The rest of the work—cutting strips of leather for vests, knitting, and crocheting—is done in the home, either their own or their neighbors'. For the crocheted leather vests, the women are given bags of leather scraps. At home they cut the leather along the edges with a pair of scissors in a continuous strip, like an apple peel.

If the work is not satisfactory, Hatice opens the stitching and they try again. If it is unsatisfactory a second time, the women are not paid and are not given any more work.

Both the type and pace of production is oriented primarily by the orders received, although minor alterations are made in the models, such as adjustments in the height of the neckline.

Prices.   Prices to the distributor vary according to the amount of crochet-work involved in the model. Osman raises prices whenever the price of leather or yarn goes up. He does not raise his prices in direct proportion to the rise in price of materials, however, but by an across-the-board 10 or 20 percent. This price rise usually is not passed on to the producers. Osman makes between 20 and 50 percent profit on what he sells, depending on the price he has managed to agree on with the merchant.

The products of Osman's atelier fetch much higher prices on the open market than are reflected in their production costs or even in Osman's prices. A large leather goods export company that purchases Osman's outfits through an intermediary has a retail outlet for tourists near the Istanbul airport. Osman's leather outfits are sold in this shop for 130,000 TL ($87) at a time when he is charging the intermediary 50,000 TL ($34) per outfit (10,000 TL [$7] if provided the materials). The women are paid 4,500 TL ($3) per outfit produced.

From a Distance: Ahmet

Piecework is sometimes organized from outside the community. Generally, however, there is some social link between the intermediary or distributor and the women hired. In this case, Ahmed, the person organizing the piecework, is the owner of a small stationery supply wholesale business in Kadıköy, a bustling business district in the old section of Istanbul.

Piecework is not Ahmed's major business but is a means of assembling items which he buys separately in bulk into individual packaged products which he sells (also wholesale) to retail stationery shops. For example, he buys bulk packages of pencil leads of various grades, plastic boxes, lids, and labels. These are sorted and assembled by pieceworkers into tiny labeled boxes of counted and graded pencil leads. Ballpoint pens are similarly assembled.

In an outlying working-class Istanbul suburb, Asiye sits on the carpet in the living room of her small apartment, painstakingly counting out fragile pencil leads, as delicate as hairs, from a large container. When she has counted ten leads, she hands them to her daughter-in-law, squatting beside her. Serap puts them into a tiny clear plastic tube. Mehmet, her eight-year-old son, puts on the tight-fitting black lid and hands it to seven-year-old Arıf, who sticks on a gold label identifying the contents and puts it into a cardboard box. Each box holds twenty-four tubes. Payment is 2 TL (less than one cent) per tube without label, and 3 TL per tube with label.

Asiye also distributes materials to five other neighboring families. Ahmet, the owner of the wholesale stationery business which distributes the pencil leads, explains, "There were some families I knew in the neighborhood that needed money. I have relatives who live close to them. I don't give the work to just anyone. I want clean work. These families I've had working for me for a year. Before that there was a family in an apartment building whose daughter didn't work and had flunked out of school. They also gave the work to their neighbors. They used to check their work and decide if they could do it or not. They apprenticed them: they went next door, taught them the work, and then recommended the family to us if they thought they could do the work well. Unfortunately, this 'pilot' or 'captain' family put the girl to work in another (paid) job, and the son started working too."

Ahmet's assistant delivers the materials to Asiye and picks up the packaged pencil leads at irregular intervals, depending on inventory needs. They are paid once a month or every ten days, or, if they specifically ask for the money, more often. Ahmet says, "If we give the money to them in a lump sum, like 100,000 TL [$67], then they can buy something for it. If we give it to them each time, they'll fritter it away. This is a sort of enforced savings." His assistant adds, "If you pay the families only a little at a time, they don't feel like they are being paid well for their work, because they spend it right away and have nothing at the end of the month; they see nothing for their labor." A tube of pencil leads sells wholesale between 50 and 280 TL, depending on the type of lead. Ahmet sells them to local shops but is trying to establish an export agreement with Saudi Arabia.

Ahmet says the families that work for him are large and have a low income. "They are ignorant," his assistant adds disapprovingly, "so they don't use birth control. Also in religion it is considered sinful, so they keep producing children." Ahmet adds that women and children do this kind of work because "it suits women more. They do fine work better. For example," he says, pointing to his typist, "in office work, women do better. Maybe it's a natural thing. Men can't type as well. Women are more patient."

The paternalistic attitude of the merchant reflects the same attitude toward women's labor (as a "natural" attribute of women and their role) as that of the piecework distributors described in this chapter as well as that of the women themselves. It provides the ideology for the devaluation of and low (and, in this case, delayed) payment for their work.

Large-Scale: Yolbaşı

In some neighborhoods hundreds of women are hired by one particular piecework distributor, who operates out of a rented storefront. These types of distributors are often outsiders to the community, although there may be some relation, as in one case in which the distributor's relatives lived near the women he hired. Business is transacted in full public view behind a storefront window so that there is no opportunity for gossip to damage the women's reputations.

In Yolbaşı, a new squatter settlement along the main highway that connects Istanbul to Ankara, the distributor is a dentist who lives and works in another part of the city. Cengiz comes into the neighborhood at regular intervals and opens the door to his storefront. Before long a line of women snakes from the door down the street; each is bringing back completed sweaters, picking up new materials, and hoping for payment.

The shop is furnished only with a long counter with two chairs and some rough shelving behind it. Basic materials are stacked on the shelves—pattern sweaters and yarns. A large pile of completed items lies on a burlap cloth on the floor. On the counter is a manual scale.

Five women wait at the counter, and a knot of women gather anxiously at the door. Fatma, who has accompanied me to meet the distributor, explains that he hasn't given out any money in months because, he says, the money from abroad hasn't reached his bank. He is a round-faced man in his late thirties, short, robust, dressed in a windbreaker over his shirt and slacks. The women waiting are of all ages, some in their teens, one woman at least fifty. A young girl behind the counter weighs the yarn before giving it to the women and also weighs the completed sweaters to be sure that the women have kept none of the yarn for themselves.

One of the women at the counter has brought three finished sweaters. Cengiz looks at them, picking one up disdainfully in his hand, and says roughly, "These are dirty and the collars are wrong. Who knitted these?" "I did," the woman answers. He tells her brusquely that she will have to do them all over again and that they should look like a sweater he has picked out of the big pile in the corner to show her. The woman complains but takes the sweaters back and leaves.

The other women are paid 10,000 or 15,000 TL each, payment for two or three completed sweaters ($3 per sweater). Cengiz continuously owes each woman an average of 30,000 to 40,000 TL ($20–$27), which is never completely paid out.

He explains to me that "the women just do this to kill time while they are watching their children and doing housework." Fatma, who is sitting near the door, agrees, "Yes, we just do it in our free time." Cengiz laughs, saying, "Some women have become professional. They do it very quickly and very well."

The women themselves, Cengiz explains, are almost all migrants from the village. "They work for lack of money; they want pots and pans; the peddler[19] passes by. They don't tell their husbands. They have an additional income of their own. They can buy a teapot or a rug. A woman teaches her daughter too. And there are homes where the daughter-in-law sits with the mother-in-law and they knit. If there are three in the family doing this, they earn more than the husband. They can make two sweaters a week," he continues. "Some do more; some do one a month. It depends on the season. They go to their villages; the place is empty and the work stops. At most, one can earn 150,000 TL [$101] a month. That is, if thirty sweaters are made—let's say by a family of three people, or by two very industrious people. Also, the family has to have no small children; the girl should be grown-up."

Cengiz began organizing the production of sweaters by piecework seven years ago, along with his father and brother in Izmir. They have a joint depot in Izmir from which the sweaters are exported to Germany and Switzerland. It took a long time to get the piecework business running smoothly, he explains. "You need dye,[20] quality control on yarn. When you sell the sweaters abroad, if the colors run, they come back and we can't give the women the money."

He tried to conduct business in two other larger neighborhoods, but one was too far from his home in Kadıköy, and the other, in which he subcontracted to another atelier, didn't work out. "We gave the yarn to an atelier there, which distributed it and collected the product. We gave the atelier 5,000 TL per sweater to give to the women, but we found out that they gave the women less. We cut off that relation. It just wasn't right. There was a terrible scene once when we came to the atelier and the women attacked us, wanting their money."

Cengiz chose Yolbaşı "with a view to the woman potential" four years ago. He had no contacts in the neighborhood. He chose this storefront because it is on a main street, rented it, and put a sign in the window advertising for knitters. He employs between 125 and

150 women, most from this neighborhood. In Yolbaşı, he says, there are also firms that hire women to do embroidery and knit leather vests, and about ten other firms doing knitting. His own firm is small compared to some in other larger neighborhoods that hire thousands of women. (Other firms such as the export company in Nişantaşı discussed above hire a thousand women or more, but production is not centralized in any particular neighborhood.)

"In the last two years such an operation has slid in and opened on every street. It's very widespread. This is because in the last two years the government has made exports much easier.[21] We don't sell anything in Turkey except to a few touristic places. We export to West Germany, Switzerland . . . they wanted more than we could make."

There is great competition among the largest piecework organizers in Istanbul who guard their labor supply and their designs jealously, even sending women as spies to discover their competitor's patterns. They try to undercut each other in the price of their products abroad. Piece-rates, on the other hand, generally vary by about 2,000 TL ($1.35) and rise only very slowly, despite rapid inflation. Too much competition in piece-rates could easily damage the market advantage that cheap labor gives these small firms. Ateliers try to create a loyal work force through a combination of paternalism, neighborhood identification, asking for a deposit (usually the rate for one sweater), and never paying out the complete amount owed the women.

Conclusion

Individual production, piecework, and the family atelier are organized in a similar way. Production is passive, in response to orders from outside of the community or from abroad. Risk is avoided in all stages of production and sale. As we shall see in the next chapter, this aversion to risk also affects the reinvestment and expansion patterns of ateliers.

The structure of each of these types of organization of labor is fluid. Women who do piecework or who produce individually in their homes may also at the same time organize other women's labor on a piecework basis or subcontract to other women. Similarly, the physical location of these production activities is fluid and may or may not involve production in the household; or production may occupy various locations at once—for example, the household and a detached or semidetached workshop for different stages of production—but involve the same people. An atelier may subcontract to another atelier, so that actual production may take place in a different part of town.

However, regardless of the specific spatial and structural configuration of production, one element common to individual production, piecework, and atelier work in the squatter areas of Istanbul is the use of family labor. If the labor is done by nonkin, the relations of production are euphemized as kin relations, emphasizing the parties' participation in the collective reciprocal exchange of labor, services, and money that characterizes kin relations in Turkey. When distributor and producers are strangers or relative strangers and of different classes, as in the case of Ahmet and Cengiz, the relations of production are disguised as paternalistic concern for the welfare of the women producers.

As a result of this ideological filter, both the women themselves and the distributors undervalue the women's labor and do not consider it to be work having a market value, although income may be derived from it. As Cengiz puts it, "Knitting sweaters is small work. Some say it's an art, but I don't see it as that. It's easy work. These are things women can do. It's merely tradition. Our women love to knit. They also need money. If we don't have them do it, they'd do it for their children and for themselves anyway."

The women themselves insist on this distinction between labor and work.[22] In their own words, they "do" (*bunu yapıyoruz*) this labor, and they "give (the product) out" (*dışarıya veriyoruz*). They do not "work" (*iş yapmak, çalışmak*), although the noun *work* (*iş*) may be used to describe their activities. This is a general noun also used to describe such activities as housework or even activity or business in general, as in *işim var* (I am busy).

Despite the devaluation of their labor as "not work," the women do occasionally ask for a higher piece-rate. This is particularly the case when the distributor is a relative outsider to the community and hires a large number of women. His relationship with the producers lacks much of the sense of mutual obligation that disguises economic activity between neighbors and kin.

Among themselves, however, the women keep to the fiction that they are not "working," only "doing" and "giving out" products to the distributor. This allows them to avoid the onus of being considered a woman who has economic dealings with strangers, a woman who has to "work," demonstrating that her husband is not able to support his family financially. This latter dishonors the family as a whole, including the woman.

In this way, the organization of women's and children's labor in family and neighborhood ateliers and as piecework constructs and reaffirms their roles as members of these social groups, that is as daughters, wives, mothers, neighbors, and so on. This allows them to contribute financially, while remaining reconciled with the moral standards of the traditional family. This conflation of labor with a woman's traditional identity is one of the factors that keep production costs low and profits high for distributors, intermediaries, merchants, and exporters.

Chapter 8
The Life Cycle of an Atelier: Yenikent

The kinship (in the broader sense of "group") logic that governs labor relations and the deployment of resources within small-scale commodity production in Istanbul can also be used to understand motivations for profit and expansion. My discussions with atelier owners and observations of their spending, growth, and investment patterns lead me to believe that their primary motivation for operating a profit-making business, beyond the basic sustenance of their families, is to acquire status markers in their community. These can be such things as a videocassette recorder, a car, their own home, and above all, the status of being boss of one's own business, regardless of how small. In other words, business is as much for social as for financial profit. The two are, of course, linked, since financial success brings with it the markers of social success and raises one's standing in the community.

This is true for the wife who participates in running the family atelier as much as for her husband. Each gains in status and influence in their respective gender group. For the woman, this status and influence is partly a result of her role as potential income provider to other women, particularly in a piecework atelier, but comes also as a result of her greater social exposure when she distributes and collects the piecework. Since the labor relationships are euphemized as social (or fictive kin) relationships, the atelier owner's wife has access to the social networks of each of the pieceworkers, thus greatly expanding her social web.

For men, the position of *patron* (employer, head, or owner of a firm or business) carries great social cachet in line with the patriarchal ideal of being a strong provider with a clear circle of authority. When the owner of the atelier described below speaks of expansion, it is this resource—social profit—that he seeks to expand, through the addition of paid employees, machines, and space.

Thus, kinship logic (in its expanded sense) leads to particular patterns of resource reinvestment and expansion that enhance the family's social status. It may also lead to business decisions that deny potential monetary gain either to avoid risk or because social profit on hand at that moment is considered sufficient in relation to the possible additional labor involved in expanding production.

In this chapter I will present a finely grained analysis of the attitudes of Osman, owner of the piecework atelier in Yenikent discussed in the previous chapter, toward reinvestment, expansion, and risk. I will then re-create the history of the atelier and follow its actual expansion and growth over the period of one year.

The transition from one level of organization and from one set of spatial arrangements to another is extremely fluid in the development of the Yenikent atelier. Complexity of organization involves such factors as whether the family is doing piecework or giving out piecework, the number of pieceworkers, and the presence or absence of salaried employees. Spatial arrangements can mean labor done in the household, labor organized from the household, labor done in and organized from a separate building nearby or in a different neighborhood, or in a building attached to but not accessible from the living quarters.

In its development, the Yenikent atelier has exhibited all of these characteristics, but without changing its basic character as a system of labor exploitation in which labor is euphemized as an expression of group identity and production is for the world market.

Reinvestment and Growth

When asked what he would like to see happen to his atelier in the future, Osman says he would like to expand it, that is, to employ salaried labor and to have more machines. The workers would all be women. "Right now the women come all the time, and some have to wait for work," he says. He would build a third floor into which the family would move, and tear down the walls on the second floor (where they live now) to make a big workshop. The bottom floor, the present location of the workshop, would be rented out or used for storage. Osman says they are saving money for building.

I ask Osman how he would go about finding new customers. He responds that he would like to go to the (international) clothing fairs. "But our capital is limited; we don't have the opportunity. We're forced to sell what we make.[1] If we don't, we don't make it." He adds that since the government won't let small firms like his export, larger firms sell what is actually his idea and his work abroad under their own name.

For example, one day two dealers from a company in Zeytinburnu that exports Osman's leather outfits to Italy and the Netherlands came to inspect their order. They looked at the finished outfits, judging how they turned out, which ones they liked, which they didn't, and decided on future orders. They had also come to give notice that they would pick up the order of 150 outfits the next day, wanting to ensure that it would be complete. They took with them the two outfits they liked best, one silver and the other black with silver spots, to show a customer they had in the shop that day.

After they left, Osman said, "They have two Italian customers in the shop, so they took two of the outfits along. They're going to deceive them. They're going to show them the outfits as if they came from their own atelier." He sighed. "Well, they're good fellows. They do what they say, and we do what we say. Anyway," he added, "they always have to worry about 'Will we be able to sell or not.' Our head, however, rests easy."

This illustrates the basic dilemma that faces small producers such as Osman: while they would like to expand and export directly, they are neither able nor willing to take the risks necessary for such an expanded venture. Expansion as pictured by Osman involves first and foremost an increase in the size and quantity of orders, for example through direct solicitation at international fairs. This would be followed by an increase in the number of machines and in salaried employees and an increase in physical workshop space. In other words, Osman's view of an expanded business does not essentially deviate from the structure of the present atelier.

While Osman and his friend Murad agree that expansion is desirable, their expectations for how expansion is to come about show that growth is reactive rather than active (or entrepreneurial). That is, growth will occur in response to larger orders. While Osman expects to and does play a role in obtaining orders, here too he expresses a desire for an outside agency to provide these orders, either the government or the chamber of commerce.

Osman complains that although the government promotes at international fairs large companies such as those that buy his leather outfits, the small atelier is not able to gain recognition. "This business is without direction (from above) [*sahipsiz*]," he adds. "The government doesn't care about helping small businesses and artisans sell things." Likewise, Osman says he needs capital so that he can join the local chamber of commerce, "which finds work for its members."

It is noteworthy that Osman uses the word *sahipsiz* to describe the situation of small businesses such as his own. The word *sahip* means owner and possessor, but also protector and master. *Sahipsiz,* literally "without a *sahip,"* means ownerless, without a protector, abandoned. *Sahip* (as a verb, with *olmak*) is the same word that is used to describe the relationship between husband and wife and between parents and child (see my discussion of this in Chapters 3 and 4). It implies ownership and control, but with a moral obligation for care and protection. This describes accurately the relationship Osman envisages between his business and the government (in the general unspecified sense of *Devlet Baba,* or Father State) and government institutions such as the chamber of commerce.

Nevertheless, Osman himself also expects to play an active role in expanding the size and number of orders, and, were it available, capital would be invested in soliciting orders (through various forms of advertisement) and in increasing production capacity (more employees, space, machines) to meet these orders. As Osman puts it, "If at the moment we had more yarn and leather, if we had stock, we would increase the staff to meet the demand." He adds, "Although there is demand, I can't buy enough material to meet it. The merchants who give orders should leave 50 percent of the final payment at the beginning, but they leave only 10 percent, so I can't buy more than a certain amount of materials. So if I have possible orders for forty women's worth of yarn per week, I only have enough money on hand to buy thirty."

In order to change this situation, he goes on, he needs money to set up. "I need two more machines, money for advertisement in newspapers and magazines that reach the producers in the leather trade, money so I can walk around giving out my card, and for brochures that show the product and the price." I ask how the new business would be different. "We would have more workers; now there are only two; there should be five or six. Now we buy 100,000 TL yarn; later we would buy 500,000 TL. What I need is capital."

Osman says he needs 5 million to 10 million TL (roughly $5,000–$10,000) to expand the atelier. He is not willing to borrow from banks. "Banks charge interest, and anyway they give only very small loans to very small artisans, not enough to make a difference." The only solution, he says, is to go into partnership with a trusted person who can invest some capital. When I ask if there are any similar businesses in the neighborhood that could join together, he says there are four or five other businesses but that they all want to go in with someone with money.

"For example," he says, "I have a friend in the leather business who has a friend in Germany. My friend sends the things to Germany and the friend there distributes them." Osman has asked his father's sister, who lives in Hamburg, to help him. He says he pointed out to her that she and her family would also profit, but she said they all worked in factories and were too busy. Osman's friend, however, has asked him for a few pieces to send to Germany with his own products.

I ask Osman what he would do if he had 50 million TL. He says he would open an atelier for ready-made clothing, not just piecework. "The point is to get big enough so I can become a member of the chamber of commerce, which finds work for its members. In order to join, one needs at least 1 million TL capital. My present capital is zero. We only produce our daily bread money."

He compares his own atelier to Murad's. "His business is only by prepayment. Someone comes; Murad takes the money, does the work. He puts about one hundred women to work knitting because he has some capital—about 10 million TL;[2] that's the crux of the matter. The capital is from his worker's pension. He works in his home and his atelier employs five people. The difference between Murad and me is that Murad can make the things without the money, and I can't make the things without getting the money for them first." "Our work is weak," Osman says later, "because we have no financial strength. We can't do anything but meet the demand. If we make a hundred (items) and ten stay home, we go under."

Nevertheless, despite his capital, Murad, like Osman, takes prepayment for his products. The additional capital is not used as a buffer to allow the atelier to take the risky step of producing on speculation, but rather to absorb the temporary cost of labor and materials until the orders are fully paid. As Osman points out above, prepayment is not 100 percent of the final price, but a fraction thereof. This leaves Osman unable to take on new orders because he cannot buy the materials needed to fill them.

Since payment for the women's labor can be postponed (sometimes for months, as in Yolbaşı, until final payment for the order is made), this does not pose a problem unless the number of women not receiving payment is very large, leading to a crisis in confidence in a particular atelier.

The women are, in a sense, giving their labor on credit. Selling (one's labor or product) on credit is risky since there is always the possibility of nonpayment. This is a problem for individual producers discussed in the previous chapter. Because their business is almost entirely with friends, neighbors, and relatives, they are not able to demand prepayment. Like the women doing piecework, individual producers operate under the fiction that they are not working, but rather participating in relations of reciprocity which require that there be no expectation of return.

Ateliers that deal with outside merchants and intermediaries, however, are able to require prepayment, since those relationships are not euphemized as kin relations (at least not to the same extent; see Chapter 6). This difference in the ideological structuring of economic relations gives the atelier owner a financial advantage, since he purchases his labor on credit but sells his product prepaid. The risk is passed on to the laborers. In the squatter areas I heard many stories of piecework distributors who left the neighborhood without paying the pieceworkers what was owed them.

Osman cannot expand his fixed labor costs by hiring salaried employees. Murad, on the other hand, is able to employ more pieceworkers as well as salaried employees because the slack in payment for orders is taken up by his capital. In other words, when capital is available, it is reinvested in growth in a limited way that does not involve risk to the capital itself.

This aversion to risking capital is enshrined in an old, dusty framed cartoon covered with cobwebs that hangs on the workshop wall by Osman's desk. It shows a worried poor man in one panel and a complacent rich man in the other. The caption under the poor man is "One who sells on credit," and under the rich man, "One who sells prepaid."

The profit that Osman accumulates from the atelier is reinvested, although in risk-free ways. He accumulates enough money from the atelier every few years to make one major purchase. Five years ago (three years after beginning the piecework business) he purchased cement blocks and cement and paid local laborers to build a workshop down the alley from his rented apartment. Two years ago he bought a car. This year he built a second-story living space above the workshop. Osman and his family were then able to stop paying rent and live there. Osman says the construction of the building cost 5 million TL (about $5,500) per floor and that it took them five years to save for the second floor (although they had also bought the car in the meantime).

The same year he added the second story, Osman also wanted to build a third floor to expand the atelier and sold the car in order to purchase materials. According to his plan, the workshop would move to the second floor, the family would live on the third floor, and the present workshop premises would be rented out or used for storage. Since the municipality did not issue a building permit, however, Osman put off this project until next year and bought another car. "This car," he told me, "is my capital."

Capital, then, is less reinvested in an atelier's growth and change than embodied in its expanding but otherwise unchanging structure. Car, house, workshop, machines, employees—all embody capital, both social and financial. The latter is risked only insofar as is necessary to accumulate the former.

The greater importance of social over financial accumulation is made clear in the following situation. During my first year of research, in addition to visiting ateliers and pieceworkers, I interviewed a number of owners of large export companies. Toward the end of the year, I was approached by one of these owners who told me that his company was expanding into the export of leather clothing and that they were looking for suitable products. They would place large orders in a continuing relationship with the producing atelier.

I quickly told the owner about Osman's atelier and product. As I had anticipated, the leather outfits were exactly what the company was looking for. The owner said I should ask Osman to call him right away and gave me both his office and home telephone numbers to pass on to Osman. I went immediately to Osman's atelier, told him about the opportunity, and gave him the telephone numbers.

A few weeks later I received a call from the export company owner who wanted to know why Osman hadn't contacted him. I went to Osman's atelier and asked him why he hadn't phoned the export company. He looked sheepish and answered, "We don't need it right now. We have enough money coming in." He had recently obtained a large steady order and had added a few smaller orders (see Phase 4 below).

Although at that point there was enough steady income to enable him to purchase materials in advance if that had become necessary and although he could have added pieceworkers at will, Osman refused this opportunity to greatly expand his business.[3] He judged his income at that particular level of risk and input of time and labor to be sufficient for his present needs. These needs, as we have seen above, are related to social status and community prestige, as well as to improving his family's comfort. Expansion is controlled by these needs, not by a desire for financial profit per se. This will be illustrated in the account given below of the life cycle of Osman and Hatice's atelier.

History of the Business

Phase 1

Until eight years ago, Hatice explained, she herself crocheted leather vests for another woman in Levent, an Istanbul neighborhood where they lived at the time. The woman made the models, hired women to copy them, and then sold them to a merchant. Osman and his neighbor Murad were without work at the time. Murad said they had seen these vests for sale in the covered bazaar and decided "We could do this too." Osman added, "The woman [Hatice] is skilled."

At first they took a few sweaters Hatice had made to shops in the bazaar, both to merchants they knew and to strangers. During the summer they took them to Kuşadası and Marmaris, resort towns, to sell to the touristic shops there. Eventually they began to get orders. They each started their own separate piecework business but borrowed materials from each other and assisted each other informally. Osman and Hatice conducted the business from their rented apartment in a squatter home nearby.

Phase 2

Five years ago, Osman had built a workshop to house the atelier. The workshop, like the family's rental home, was an "unofficial" building and had been torn down several times by the municipality and rebuilt. At the time of my first visit at the beginning of 1987, however, Osman said that the papers were in the process of being approved and when that occurred he would build his own apartments on top of the workshop. The workshop itself represented capital since it could be rented out for 70,000 TL ($77) a month.

The atelier produced a variety of products such as leather knitted vests, tops (which were referred to as T-shirts) and skirts made of leather pieces crocheted together, and occasionally, knitted sweaters in response to small orders from merchants in the covered bazaar, who cater primarily to tourists. Osman elicited these orders by bringing sample models to the merchants.

He prepared the leather pieces in the workshop with the help of his daughter Emine. His wife Hatice passed out materials to the women who came for work, collected the finished products, and checked their quality. Osman kept a log of the women's names, the materials they had taken, and the amount owed them. Production varied according to the orders Osman had elicited that month.

A hole-punching machine had been newly acquired just before my first visit. Osman had made it himself from an old treadle sewing machine that had broken down, making his own parts (except for the leather punches) with metal scissors and other simple tools. Before that, they had made holes with a hand punch, a much slower process. With a hand punch, they were able to produce the ready leather for ten T-shirts a day, Osman explained, but now with the machine they could punch enough for a hundred a day. Osman made regular trips to Bursa by car, about a three-hour trip, to purchase yarn directly from a factory, since it was cheaper. He did not, however, buy it in bulk but rather went every week if necessary to purchase only the materials needed for a particular order. He did this so that there would be no excess yarn that they would perhaps be unable to use.

At the time, the family lived in a small rental apartment in a squatter building down a muddy alley behind the main road. The home was sparsely furnished, with two beds in a narrow sitting room lit by a single window at the rear. A tiny windowless kitchen and bedroom opened off the sitting room, and a small bathroom off the hall. The largest room was the little-used parlor, which was furnished with a shabby couch and two armchairs painted white and gilded, a large dining table, and a blue painted wooden cabinet that housed glass bric-a-brac. The floor was adorned with a cheap machine-made carpet.

Phase 3

Within two months of my first visit, the atelier had changed the orientation of its production to suit a substantial steady order from a large export company (which exported to the United States). Osman now sold to four merchants who acted as intermediaries for boutiques, summer resorts, and export companies (exporting also to Germany, the Netherlands, and Italy).

Before this, the atelier had produced small amounts of a variety of products. Three or four pieces at a time were sold to individual merchants. With the new orders they began to produce about one hundred pieces a month, primarily the two-piece outfits composed of leather diamonds connected by crocheted panels, for export.

They also began to use a better quality yarn, bought from a different company, although they still went to Bursa to purchase it. Osman said they now bought a bit more at once, especially basic colors. But looking on the storage shelves I saw there were still fewer than twenty skeins of those colors (brown and black) on hand. The new yarn was 100 percent viscose rayon and cost 200–300 TL more per skein, but Osman said it was worth the extra cost because it improved the quality of the merchandise. Also, Osman explained, the export company that placed the order had reported that American buyers inspect the quality of the merchandise very minutely—unlike German buyers, for example.

The export company's intermediary provided his own good-quality leather, precut into diamond shape. Fifty large pieces and ten smaller ones, enough for one skirt, were delivered to Osman bound between triangles of cardboard. Osman punched holes in the leather. Each woman who came to the atelier to get work was given one of these packages and three hundred grams of yarn. It took a woman two days' work, five hours a day, to complete a skirt. For this she was paid 2,500 TL. For the leather top, which also required that she crochet three hundred grams of yarn, she was paid 2,000 TL, a total of 4,500 TL (about $5) per outfit.

The women were paid after Osman received the money from the intermediary, usually at the end of the month when he came to pick up the order. The women then came all on one day at the end of the month and told Osman how many pieces they had made. He checked the figure in his ledger, put the money in an envelope, and handed it to them.

Phase 4

I did not visit the atelier for three months. When I returned, I discovered that the neighborhood had changed to such an extent that I could not immediately get my bearings, even though the bus stopped only a short way down the street from the atelier. The points of reference I had used before had all been visible from the bus stop: the mosque and, across the street, the shed that housed a vegetable shop built onto the front of a cement block house. In the back of this house, down a narrow alleyway, had been the workshop.

This time, when I got out of the bus, I recognized only the mosque. The house behind the vegetable seller's shack was completely gone. The workshop building, once I recognized it, had a second story. Furthermore, the entire neighborhood was littered with new houses and two- and three-story apartment buildings under construction.

After a few moments of disorientation, I decided that this was the same vegetable shop and asked the man and young girls inside for directions to Osman's atelier. The man pointed to the alley, and I disappeared down it between the gray cement walls. When I entered the workshop I saw the daughter, Emine, and another teenage girl working at two hole-punching machines. I saw right away that not only the neighborhood had changed in the few months I had been away.

I chatted with the two girls until Osman arrived. I told him about the hard time I had finding the workshop because of all the new construction. He said that about a month ago everyone had started building at once, including himself, but that the municipality had now forbidden it. Many places were standing but not finished. "Some may even be torn down because they were built without permission," he added.

Changes in the atelier included a second manual hole-punching machine that he had bought secondhand two months before from a downtown dealer. "There is a lot of work," Osman said. "People we know find us and give us bigger orders. Now five firms give us orders. Two of them are new ones; one is near Izmir, in Kuşadası."[4] He was going to Kuşadası soon, to make his wares known.

He complained that since he was without a car, it was difficult to get around. They had sold the car to build the third story of the house, he said, but the municipality would not permit the construction, and they now had to buy another car. They probably would not be able to build until the following year, he concluded.

Osman and Emine took me back up the alley to the entrance of the new floor. They had moved here from the rental apartment down the road. The new house looked much more prosperous, although it was only slightly larger than the previous apartment. There was a bedroom for the parents, a newly furnished parlor, and a sitting room which was the focus of nearly all household activity outside the kitchen. Meals were eaten there, and it was used during the day to watch television or videos and to receive guests. All four children slept in the sitting room at night.

The kitchen was not large but spacious by Turkish standards. Osman proudly pointed out the brown tile counter and stainless steel sink, which he said had cost 28,000 TL ($31). The painted cabinet that had formerly been in the parlor was now in the kitchen and contained jars of foodstuffs. There was a large refrigerator and, under the counter, aluminum pots of various sizes; on the shelf was enough plastic dishware for the family and a few guests. The bathroom was fairly large and tiled in the same brown tile as the kitchen counter, with a Turkish toilet, a small cylindrical semiautomatic washing machine, and a blue plastic stool by a shower hose attached to the wall—a Turkish bath. The room looked quite modern and indeed was much nicer than the bathroom in my own rental apartment.

When we went out the front door, I noticed to the left a room facing the street with a large plate glass window. It had its own entrance to the street and had no doorway connecting it to the inside of the house. Osman told me that this was eventually to be a showroom for his products and a place to receive customers. The workshop would be a workplace only. When he built the third story, he continued, the entire second floor, where they now lived, would be converted into workshop and showroom. He planned to rent out the bottom floor where the workshop was now located. The third floor would be entirely living space, 330 square feet—as opposed to their present home's 230 square feet of living space.

Back in the workshop, I noticed that the leather pieces were now embossed and also in mixed colors (black on white, or black with gold, silver, etc.). Osman said that they bought some of the pieces themselves from the clothing ateliers but that most of the leather still came precut from the people who gave the orders. He still got the yarn from Bursa but since he had no car, he gave an order and "road money" to friends who go there regularly.

Another innovation was the addition of about fifty outfits made on speculation. These were put on a separate shelf for the buyers who dropped in to give orders and who asked for extra pieces to take away with them right away. With the extra pieces, Osman was always ready for an extra order. He had them made up "whenever he felt like it," using extra yarn and leather.

Phase 5

Two months later, the transfer of the office to the room built onto the front of the house was complete. The workshop on the bottom floor was now used only for production. The merchants and intermediaries came to the front office to place and pick up orders. Osman also received his male friends there when they stopped by to chat. The workshop had become a female domain.

This separation of function and space by gender in the atelier was reinforced by the physical location and geographic context of the office and the workshop. The workshop was on the bottom floor with its only entrance at the back of the house from a narrow muddy back lane that led to other lanes giving access to homes scattered at the back of the main road. The lanes were used by the women to visit each others' homes. The only immediate access to the workshop from the main road in front was along a narrow alley between the blind walls of two buildings. The office, on the other hand, faced the main paved road along which the city bus traveled. Visible from the office were the mosque and coffeehouse down the street, both also male territory.

The new office was a large bright room with only one entrance and faced fully in front with a glass pane. It contained a desk, a counter, and shelves around two sides. On the shelves were piles of the various types of leather outfits the workshop produced. There was also a shelf full of sweatshirts with a cartoon on the front. Osman said he had gotten them from an export company that had a surplus. He had bought them for 5,000 TL and sold them for 6,000 TL each. However, he explained that he did not pay the export company for them until he had sold them. The sweatshirts were for local neighborhood consumption, since "Turks don't wear the other things" he makes.

On the workshop shelves I noticed extra unsorted pieces of cut leather (in addition to the neat piles of precut pieces brought by the merchants). I also noticed larger quantities of colored yarn, ten to fifteen skeins as opposed to the usual five or six. Osman explained, "We have lots of orders now so I decide on my own colors and buy materials ahead. We buy if we have lots of money, not just because the prices go up."[5]

There were three rolls of white cloth bands on the shelves, indications of the atelier's export orientation. The bands could be cut to make labels that said, "Made in Turkey" (in English), "Echt Leder" (Genuine Leather), and 1, 2, or 3 (sizes). There was another innovation: a roll of cord for the skirts—a thin knitted strip to make the waists adjustable. Some of the leather tops now had beaded flowers on them and others had sleeves.

On the shelf I also saw a few men's jackets made of heavy solid leather with no crochet. The leather was poor quality and had been colored to achieve a more "modern" look. When I asked about the jackets, Osman explained that he had subcontracted the work to another atelier. The atelier was in Zeytinburnu and belonged to a friend, an Afghan who ran a workshop staffed entirely by Afghan women and children. Osman bought the leather, gave it to the atelier, then took the final product. The atelier used its own thread and lining. He pointed to the vest he was wearing, a thick suede sleeveless vest lined with white fleece, "This was made by the same atelier."

The materials for the leather jacket cost Osman 20,000 TL. He gave 5,000 TL to the other atelier, and then sold the jacket for 30,000 TL—a profit of 5,000 TL. He said he had sold fifty of them in a month. He had an order for them now and has said he would provide them once a month. The vest was for government highway workers when they worked outside in the cold. He said he had sold two hundred of them at 20,000 TL apiece. He paid the atelier 15,000 TL for each vest.

Although it was not possible for me to check Osman's figures, even spread out over two months this subcontracting arrangement had brought Osman a substantial additional income of 1,250 million TL ($1,388)—*without* any direct organization of labor and production on his part. Osman had now taken on both the role of producer (or organizer of production) and of intermediary. The actual labor was still done by women and children in workshops where the organization of labor was based on family and/or, in this case, regional/ethnic group ties.

Conclusion

The Yenikent atelier grew out of Hatice's piecework for another merchant. Using Hatice's work to obtain orders, Osman first began organizing piecework from their home, then built a workshop nearby. Later, he built their living quarters on top of the workshop and eventually added a separate office. This spatial innovation separated the male function of selling from the female function of producing. He added a young girl as a salaried employee in the workshop, bought a second machine, and planned to build a larger workshop area. He also expanded and oriented his production to meet larger orders. In addition, he became an intermediary for the products of an atelier in another part of town and began to sell a few products on the local market as well as producing for export.

Despite all these innovations, Osman was careful not to incur any risk.[6] Even the decision to make some T-shirts on speculation was in response to regular requests by visiting merchants for immediately available merchandise. With this cautious expansion, the family became more prosperous, moving to their own home and purchasing new furniture. Nevertheless, when offered the opportunity to greatly expand production on a regular basis, Osman refused, choosing instead to proceed in a manner that balanced risk with "socially sufficient" income.

In the next chapter, I will conclude by situating this type of production within the debate about the precise constitution of small-scale commodity production. This debate revolves around topics discussed in the previous chapters: the role of family labor, the household, and economic rationality in determining the makeup of piecework production; the role (if any) that profit maximization and accumulation play in the life cycle of an Istanbul atelier. Here, I will tie together the structure of small-scale commodity production for the world market and the kinship logic of economic practice within the context of small-scale production in Istanbul squatter districts.

Chapter 9
Kinship and Capitalism

Although family labor is central to the definition of small-scale commodity production, very little attention has been paid to the power relations and ideology that underlie internal labor processes, particularly with regard to the division of labor by gender. This criticism has been leveled against orthodox Marxist analysis by feminist and other scholars working within the Marxist tradition.[1] Recent rethinking of the role of small-scale commodity production[2] under capitalism has generated efforts to broaden classical Marxist analysis by examining the effects of relations of domination by age and gender within the family/household on its articulation with the capitalist system. Despite a number of important advances in conceptualizing relations within the family/household, such relations generally have remained divorced from "market relations" beyond the border of the household. Family relations are treated not as capitalist relations but as a mediating phenomenon between the producing group and the capitalist system, that is, as an adjunct to capitalist relations of production beyond the household or derived from the household's class position. Despite attention paid to family/household relations, with some exceptions (cf. Lem 1991; Mies 1986b), most analyses do not address issues of ideology and power within the internal production process itself.

This restrictive view of relations within the producing group forms a barrier to understanding certain characteristics of small-scale commodity production that appear in the Istanbul context, such as the importance of reciprocal ties in determining the relations of production within the group and the ability of the producing group to expand spatially beyond the household and beyond the family in terms of membership without changing its basic structure.

These characteristics of small-scale production in Istanbul can be better understood if the relations internal to the group are theorized as part of the capitalist process, rather than as an adjunct to it. As

Friedmann points out with regard to family farms in the American Midwest, family enterprises exist not as a separate mode of production under capitalism (and articulated with it) but as enterprises within branches of capitalist economies (1987:248). Small-scale production in this view has both an external relation to the capitalist order as well as internal relations that are specific to capitalism. This discussion is an attempt to specify the internal labor process of a group of urban commodity producers linked to the world market.

As we have seen in this account of the structure of small-scale commodity production in Istanbul squatter districts and the cultural logic within which it is embedded, such production is both a capitalist enterprise with links to the world market that exploits labor on the basis of class, age, and gender and a means of creating and maintaining group solidarity. In other words, small-scale production in Istanbul can be understood by reference to two ideological orders—that of capitalism and that of the social group.

In the examples given in the preceding chapters the producing group was able to expand spatially beyond the household and even employ nonfamily workers without changing its basic structure. Any changes in location and membership of the producing group are bridged by a particular kinship logic based on reciprocity and obligation that also pervades social and economic practice in Turkey in general. These open-ended reciprocal relations among group members form a type of social agreement for mutual assistance which provides for long-term security and which takes kinship as its idiom.

I suggest that such relations of reciprocity within commodity-producing groups in Istanbul are not distinct from capitalist relations of production. Rather, I argue that these group relations (modeled as kin relations, whether the members are actual kin or not) act as relations of production within the commodity-producing group and that, therefore, the extraction of surplus value from the labor of women producers occurs within the producing group itself as well as at the point of contact between the group and the capitalist market, as is assumed in Marxist theory. In other words, the transactional system within which small-scale production occurs is characterized by *both* market forces and collective reciprocity. The extraction of profit proceeds on the basis of the collective reciprocity, while the position of the group as a whole within the market (that is, its class characteristics) provides the conditions for an extraction of profit based on market coercion.

The idea that kinship relations can function as social relations of production has been suggested by Godelier with regard to certain types of noncapitalist societies. In these societies, kinship relations "assume the functions of determining access to and control over the means of production and the social product for the groups and individuals comprising a particular type of society, and organizing the process of production as well as the process of distribution of products" (1988:28). The study of small-scale production and family enterprise in Istanbul shows that this idea can be extended to apply to certain types of economic enterprise in a capitalist society as well. Here, profit is extracted from the labor of some group members by others through relations of production that emphasize open-ended reciprocity and social solidarity.

There remains the question of how to conceptualize such a coexistence within the group of individual acquisition and exploitation on the one hand and the primacy of collective reciprocity, solidarity, and mutual security on the other. I refer later on in the chapter to a two-sphere model of transactional systems developed by Parry and Bloch (1989) for understanding similar seemingly contradictory spheres of exchange in precapitalist societies. First, however, let us consider in more detail recent attempts to incorporate family/ household relations in Marxist theories of small-scale commodity production.

Small-Scale Production in a Capitalist Context

Citing evidence from studies of small-scale commodity production in various parts of the world, Marxist theoreticians have challenged two basic assumptions and projections about the relation of small-scale production to capitalism (cf. Bernstein 1986; Bromley and Gerry 1979; Gibbon and Neocosmos 1985). *1.* Small-scale commodity production is a transitional stage within capitalism and will disappear with the development of capitalism and the proletarianization of the work force. *2.* It is a form of nonwage labor which "subsidizes" capital accumulation and produces cheap labor power. That is, it is a form of disguised wage labor but is not in itself a capitalist form of production.

Revisionists argue that small-scale commodity production as it is practiced both in developing and developed countries today exists in an environment conditioned by capitalist relations and should therefore be seen as a form of production specific rather than prior to or separate from capitalist production. In grappling with the exact constitution of small-scale production under capitalism, however, these authors have had to locate within their definitions certain conditions of existence that are not analyzable solely through the logic of the market (Friedmann 1980, 1986; Bernstein 1986). Since the household and family labor are central elements of Marxist definitions of small-scale commodity production, these too must be situated theoretically within the capitalist environment. However, as Feldman points out, "studies which identify the household as a locus of production may ignore both the heterogeneity of household organization and the gender division of labor" and their significance in shaping production and consumption practices (1991:66).

Relations of domination such as those based on gender and age, which are fundamental to family/household relations, have been subject to discussion, but primarily within the context of social class and the relation of capital to labor. Despite their interest in the cultural mechanisms of intrafamilial exploitation and the relation of these cultural mechanisms to small-scale commodity production, Marxist theorists situate this interest within what is basically a materialist definition of small-scale production, which requires that it be defined either by wage labor or by the absence of wage labor[3] (and by the unity of capital and labor), depending on the particular form of production and its articulation with the capitalist mode of production. In the latter case, while relations external to the household are commodified and labor can be sold, it is assumed that relations within the household are not mediated by commodities and labor is unified with capital. This leads to "an untenable dualism in which the household and relations within it are divorced from 'market relations' beyond" (Lem 1991:106).

If relations of production within small-scale production are based on ownership by the same group of the means of production *and* labor power, as in the traditional Marxist formulation, it is not possible to conceptualize an internal conflict and the extraction of surplus value from the labor of one member by another. It is for this reason that Marxist scholars, when writing about the division of labor or gender domination within the family, find it necessary to conceptualize these as phenomena related to but separate from small-scale production.

Harriet Friedmann, for example, sees family enterprise as having a dual nature as both "enterprise" and "family." Small-scale commodity production is both a set of (capitalist) relations of production and a set of class-specific family/household relations (1986).[4] She also explicitly excludes from the category of commodity production any production that is reproduced (all or in part) through noncommodity relations, defined as "'direct reciprocal ties, both horizontal and vertical' through which access to means of production and subsistence is obtained" (Bernstein 1986:14).

As Martha Roldán writes, "The theoretical 'lens' of the PCP [petty commodity production] model finds it almost impossible to focus upon relations of domination which are not directly expressed in terms of class" (1985:253). The tendency of Marxist analyses to relegate the sexual division of labor to second place, notes Roldán,

> constitutes the great theoretical *weakness* of an approach which, even though it superficially recognizes the role of family relations in the reproduction of the small workshop, enterprise or home-based, industrial outworking activity based on unpaid family labor, it nevertheless persists in focusing its analytical attentions on the *relatively insignificant incidence* of wage-labour in these activities. (Ibid.; emphasis in original)

As an intended corrective to this tendency, she cites recent studies of women's labor in Latin America that stress the importance of the household and the domestic environment as factors which condition women's participation in the labor force. The domestic unit is seen as a mediating factor between macrostructural processes and the incorporation of family members into the labor market. In Roldán's view, the theoretical advance of this over the classic Marxist analysis is that it concentrates on the family group as mediator of labor rather than as an aggregate of individual suppliers of labor. She stresses the need for a formulation of "the dialectical relationship between the sphere of labour and that of the household" (1985:282).

Roldán adds the important recognition that the family does not maximize its welfare as a complementary whole, but rather that the family itself is a contradictory institution. The family is a locus of class domination and subordination by gender and age, but it is also a source of solidarity, mutual aid, and protection in times of crisis. Friedmann also notes the contradiction within the commodity-producing family between the patriarchal direction of labor and the "cooperative and egalitarian self-direction of work" (1986:55).

What is indicated by the descriptions of small-scale commodity production in Istanbul is a recognition of the role of such contradictory family/household relations not only in the reproduction of small-scale production but also in production itself. This has been realized in part in the work of Winnie Lem, in which she differentiates ownership of property and labor within the commodity-producing family by gender and generation. "In these respects, it becomes possible to speak of a 'class-like' relationship prevailing in the domestic domain" (1991:111). Several writers also have suggested that patriarchal relations in the family that lead to the subordination of women's and children's labor to the family production project constitute a basis for capital accumulation (Mies, Bennholdt-Thomsen, and Werlhof 1988; Cohen 1988).

The various levels of organization of production indicated by the Istanbul data are encompassed with difficulty within Marxist parameters for small-scale commodity production. For example, while it is theoretically possible to consider individual production as a form of small-scale commodity production (Bernstein 1986:14), the idea of property and labor (and the implied conflict of interest) internalized within a single person is problematic and not pursued in the literature. The family/household is more amenable to this formulation, particularly if one assumes the possibility of internal conflicts of interest along the lines of gender and age. However, these fault lines generally are not theorized as part of the process of small-scale production, but rather appear as a factor mediating between the individual within the group and the capitalist market.

Location of production also is problematic because, as the Istanbul examples show, production can be located either in the household or without. Production itself is mobile, and within a short period of time the location of production and all other atelier activities can move fluidly between the household and one or more separate locations. In other words, the household, as a location of production, is not a necessary feature of small-scale production. Furthermore, not only is family labor not necessarily coterminous with the household (cf. Lem 1991), but the concept of family labor may also include the labor of nonkin who share in relations of production predicated upon group membership.

The issue of labor remuneration in small-scale production (and the employer-employee relations that are presumed to accompany a wage relation) is too complex an issue to be dealt with merely by noting the existence or absence of a wage. In the Istanbul ateliers the relations of production are predicated upon reciprocal ties— that is, they are structured as noncommodity relations—whether a monetary wage is paid or not.

Capitalist exploitation of the women's labor, moreover, is not in question, since surplus value is clearly extracted from their labor by intermediaries and merchants, both locally and internationally. Again, this is the case whether the women are paid a wage or not. This vacillation between paid and unpaid labor does not indicate movement between different forms of production, but rather expresses the equivalence of relations of production based on the ideology of group membership, regardless of whether a wage is paid or not.

I believe it creates a false dichotomy to argue that since capital and labor are combined in commodity-producing households using unpaid family labor, there is no capitalist exploitation (other than in terms of class) in such households, but only exploitation on the basis of gender and age. To explain the Istanbul data, an expanded position is needed that accounts for capitalist exploitation (extraction of surplus value) within a unitary producing group and that broadens the definition of the commodity-producing group so that it is not necessarily coterminous with household or family. This is only possible through a reformulation of the notion of family as a unity of labor and capital.

Kinship Relations of Production

To summarize the discussion so far, in the Marxist tradition small-scale commodity production has been theorized as aggregates of individuals each owning their own labor power. Recent interventions by Friedmann and Roldán have focused on the nature of the group (family/household) in an attempt to understand patterns of domination within the group. However, the relations of production within small-scale production remain undifferentiated within this analysis because the contradictions within the group (such as gender- and age-based hierarchies) are conceived of as an adjunct to and influence on the relation between labor and capital, which is seen to be a given. The effect of such contradictions on relations of production within the household has been explored in the work of Lem (1991), Mies (1986b), and Cohen (1988).

Each of these attempts at theorizing the processes internal to the family/household has had to grapple with the issue of ownership of labor and of the means of production. In Marxist theory, the particular configuration of the unity of capital and labor within an individual or group is used as the basis for defining small-scale production and for fixing the parameters of inclusion. This leads to the question of how to account for the extraction of surplus value from the labor of some by others in the group, when the group is defined as an aggregate of individuals within which labor and capital is unified.

The theoretical lacuna that emerges, particularly in the light of the present study of small-scale producers in Istanbul, is a way of theorizing the contradictions internal to the commodity-producing group in relation to the production of commodities itself, rather than as an adjunct to it. As an attempt at a solution, I suggest that the relations of production in small-scale production in Istanbul are *not* based on aggregate group ownership of labor power and the means of production. Rather, they are based on the right of the group to have use of (usufruct rights in) the means of production and labor power of its individual members.

Thus, while group members act as a productive group providing solidarity and security for its members, this formulation also leaves room for individual ownership of the means of production and of labor power, a contradiction between labor and capital within the group and consequent exploitation of one member by the other. This individual ownership is disguised and in fact superseded in determining the relations of production among members by the primacy of collective reciprocity over market relations. The group, in other words, acts in solidarity while individual members pursue personal profit.

This coexistence of exploitation and social synergy forms the core of James Scott's analysis of "everyday" forms of resistance by Malaysian peasants against exploitation by a class of elites. Scott discusses how economic domination of the peasant by the landlord is euphemized as generosity and friendship. He suggests that this euphemization of economic power is achieved through the partial socialization[5] of the profits of cultivation. That is, a portion of the crop and the proceeds from it are given by the landlord to the peasant in the form of gifts, feasts, and so on.

Scott is careful to point out that "there has of course never been any socialization of the ownership of the means of production" (1985:308). Bottomore (1983:447), however, allows that two forms of socialization involve the transformation of the means of production into group property (in the form of small-scale agricultural production and service cooperatives) and into the property of an entire society (in the form of self-managing workers' cooperatives).

While in the Marxist formulation these types of socialization involve particular sets of worker collectivities under capitalism, the philosophical root of the concept lies in a fundamentally different attitude of people to objects (and to other people).

> The concept of private property has two meanings. One is private ownership of the means of production. The other is a general attitude to life characterized by the desire to *own* an object (or a person reduced to a thing). . . . The abolition of private property in this general philosophical sense involves an entirely different

socialization of human individuals, characterized by a full development of creative capacities, of the *sense of being* rather than the sense of *having*. (Ibid.; emphasis in original)

Scott focuses on a particular construction of social relations between peasant and elite in which the landowner manipulates his profit to create a social bond with the peasant, an incomplete form of socialization. This formulation of the relationship revolves around *having* and therefore highlights the struggle of the peasantry to avoid giving to, and to maintain getting from, the landowner. Thus he remarks that the charges the poor make against the rich are almost always related to a decline in the gifts, alms, and so on expected from the elite.

The situation in Istanbul, however, is characterized less by resistance than by acquiescence and, indeed, by a heightening of solidarity between "exploiter" and "exploited." It is this difference in what is clearly also a moral economy of production that must be explored.

In the Istanbul case, I have suggested that the means of production, while owned by individuals, are also in a sense (in terms of usufruct rights) group property. Through the contribution of labor to the group and the provision to the group of access to the means of production and consequent opportunities for income, the identity of each individual is submerged in the group identity. In other words, the individual (along with his or her labor and property) *is* the group.

While this "sense of being" does not completely replace the "sense of having," it does adequately characterize the "general attitude to life" of the workshop and piecework workers described in this study. Collective reciprocity—the requirement and benefit of group membership—euphemizes and takes precedence over the extraction of profit.

The Moral Economy of Capitalist Small Enterprise

Parry and Bloch (1989), in their introduction to a collection of articles dealing with the role of money in various precapitalist systems of exchange, provide a useful way of looking at this seeming contradiction between exploitation and the primacy of collective reciprocity within the group. They conclude that what is similar across different cultures about the pattern of meaning surrounding monetary transactions is "the relationship between a cycle of short-term exchange which is the legitimate domain of individual—often acquisitive—activity, and a cycle of long-term exchanges concerned with the reproduction of the social and cosmic order" (1989:2).

It has been widely argued that in precapitalist societies the economy is "embedded" in society and the pursuit of individual material gain is discouraged, with collective goals being primary over those of the individual. The influence of this point of view on Marxist definitions and redefinitions of small-scale production is clear. Household production, as a form of nonwage labor, is considered to be outside the capitalist sphere of material acquisition, which is predicated upon a conflict between labor and capital. Friedmann's and Roldán's reformulations of this position attempt to break down the notion that the family/household is characterized primarily by collective goals.

Parry and Bloch suggest, however, that in precapitalist societies there exist two spheres of economic activity, one which allows individual acquisition and one which is concerned with the cycle of long-term reproduction. The former is ideologically articulated with and subordinated to the latter sphere. Goods derived by means of individual acquisition are converted within a matrix of meaning unique to each culture into elements of a "moral economy" that ensures the long-term reproduction of the social order.

Parry and Bloch are concerned to show that money and market exchange can exist embedded within traditional moral values in precapitalist societies and do not necessarily subvert them. My study of small production in Istanbul suggests that this may also be the case in capitalist societies. I would argue that a moral economy can exist in capitalist enterprise involving the exchange of money and that this can be explained within the capitalist context without needing to posit the influence or existence of remnants of precapitalist attitudes and practices.

A major theme in Western discourse about money has been "that it represents an intrinsically revolutionary power which inexorably subverts the moral economy of 'traditional' societies" (ibid.: 12). For Marx, since money is the medium for market exchange, it accompanies and promotes the growth of individualism and the destruction of unitary communities. According to this view, the exchange of commodities tends to dissolve bonds of personal dependence between members of a community, bonds which had been present under a system of production for use in which materials, labor, and services were exchanged directly.

However, Parry and Bloch introduce a series of articles which show the importance of money and market exchange in many "traditional," precapitalist economies which had previously been characterized as nonmonetary. The authors attempt to demonstrate that "the index of monetisation is not a reliable index of the atrophy of the 'moral economy'" (1989:8).

In discussing what has often been referred to as a precapitalist economic mentality, Parry and Bloch argue that this refers merely to different cultural constructions of money. I would add that where the group is the primary index of social life, elements of economic life—like money and relations of production—derive their meaning and their *efficacy* from the same cultural logic that informs social life in general.

Parry and Bloch shift the focus away from the meanings of money to the meanings of entire transactional systems. Doing so forces a reconsideration of the meanings of such money-related concepts as wage and relations of production (whose meanings in Marxist analysis resonate with the cultural logic of the individualist West) within the cultural logic of the particular capitalist society in which they are found.

For example, Parry and Bloch examine the cultural construction of money within our own individualistic society. In our culture, money signifies a sphere of impersonal, transitory, amoral, and calculatingly economic relationships, a domain where moral precepts and personal relations have no natural place. This impersonality of money, they argue, makes it inappropriate as a gift in our society, but this is not the case in other societies where money is embedded within a different cultural logic. Parry and Bloch conclude that where the economy is not seen as a separate and amoral domain, monetary relations are not likely to be represented as the antithesis of bonds of kinship and friendship. In such societies, money may be appropriate as a gift. They note perceptively that *"our* ideology of the gift has been constructed in antithesis to market exchange" (1989:9).

In this study I have attempted to demonstrate the possibility that a moral economy can exist under capitalist conditions and, taking Parry and Bloch's ideas about the relation of monetary to social relations one step further, that monetary relations may be represented *as* bonds of kinship and friendship under these conditions.

Among the small-scale commodity producers in Istanbul, money is not fetishized as a commodity that breeds money (see the discussion of social profit in previous chapters), nor is money as capital "ideologically transformed into the source of production, reducing the workers to mere appendages, making it appear only right and proper that capital should reap its 'just reward'" (ibid.:6). Rather, money is embodied in social life itself, as part of a system of reciprocal exchange. Likewise, capital is embodied as social value—house, car, status, and so on. The "just reward" of the capitalist is defined in terms of social justice.

Labor Given, Labor Sold: Lawful Profit in the Marketplace

In line with the primacy of collective reciprocity over market forces in determining the relations of production, individual profit within the Istanbul commodity-producing group is as much a social as a financial phenomenon. It must be lawful profit, profit that by definition is derived from the freely given labor of other group members rather than through the coercion of market laws.

In other words, relations of exploitation within the group are based on the same principles of reciprocity and indebtedness that build group solidarity and security. Both group solidarity and individual profit are derived from the usufruct rights of the group in the resources of its members. Relations of domination are also at the same time relations of group solidarity. Giving labor and giving work (and extracting *legitimate* profit) solidify relations of solidarity *while* providing the mechanism for the extraction of surplus value (in the form of gender- and age-based contradictions) by some group members from the labor of others.

In the Marxist formulation, relations of domination within the group are able to be theorized only with difficulty as part of the process of small-scale production. The difficulty arises because the analysis of the latter as a form of capitalist production is predicated upon contradiction and conflict between ownership of the means of production and ownership of labor power—that is, on class conflict. By this definition, such conflict is absent within family production. Extraction of surplus value, then, occurs at the point of contact between the group and its capitalist environment, rather than at a point within the group. Within the group, there is domination and exploitation on the basis of gender and age, but this exploitation generally has not been theorized in the Marxist model as part of capitalist production.

Having acknowledged the possibility of internal contradictions within the family and the necessity of analyzing them to understand small-scale production under capitalism (as do Lem, Friedmann, and Roldán), then it is necessary to go one step further and to theorize them *within* the parameters of Marxist economics. To do this it is necessary to identify the root of internal conflict in the relations of production within the group. These relations are not undifferentiated (unity of property and labor), as they appear in the Marxist model. They are rather predicated upon a different understanding of ownership. (See the discussion of economic ownership and usufruct rights in Chapter 7.)

Each individual in the group contributes one or more of the following: labor, access to machines and materials, remuneration in the form of money, services, or goods. The pieceworkers and atelier workers contribute labor. The atelier owners (the wife may be co-owner, although merchandising and management decisions are made by the outward-facing husband) contribute their labor and money and give access to machines and materials to other group members. This access opens to the group members the possibility of receiving money from the atelier owners. The workers are paid in cash per piece produced, a small wage for atelier work, socially defined wealth such as wedding expenses, or in indebtedness for future services.

The money accumulated by the atelier owners is *legitimate* profit. That is, it is profit which has been obtained in a manner whereby that which has profited a person was freely given without expectation of return. Unlawful profit is profit which has been obtained through coercion. In other words, profit is obtained within the commodity-producing group through the extraction of surplus value, but it is obtained as a result of collective reciprocity rather than on the basis of the coercion of market forces that drive the individual (or group) to sell his or her labor power to the capitalist owner of the means of production.

Labor and remuneration are understood in the Istanbul context to be freely given within a larger set of mutual obligation and reciprocity. This "enchantment" of market forces provides an explanation for a number of attributes of small-scale production that have until now needed to be theorized outside of capitalist production. These attributes include what have been called precapitalist attitudes toward accumulation (preferring to invest in status rather than growth), the organization of labor by age and gender, and the persistence of patriarchal values even under capitalist conditions (Friedmann 1986).

In Marxist analyses, the group (which is always the family/household) appears to function as an autonomous economic entity with regard to the extraction of surplus value in the capitalist market (with the possibility of internal contradictions that nevertheless are not theorized as being part of capitalist production). I argue here that these market forces operate within the group as well, but that they are obscured by an ideology of group obligation and mutual indebtedness. This is the same ideology which euphemizes capitalist economic practice in Turkey (see Chapter 6).

As well as a division of labor (as between male and female) in the group, there is a division of function—female production and male marketing, for example (although this particular division applies only to piecework ateliers, not to ateliers producing, for example, shoes or metalwork, where the labor is done by men and boys). More important is the division between those providing labor and those extracting surplus value from that labor. In the case of the family atelier, the group (in the name of the individual) extracts surplus value from the labor of individuals. In the case of piecework, the owners of the atelier extract surplus value from the pieceworkers.

However, all parties consider themselves as having obtained a lawful profit. The pieceworkers are not coerced into providing labor; indeed they insist they do not "sell" their labor but "give" it freely. The money they receive, while it is literally in exchange for piecework labor, is part of a wider system of reciprocity. That is, the money paid for piecework is a marker of social relations devoid of naked economic (unlawful, profit-oriented) motives.

The relations of production within small-scale commodity production, then, can be theorized on the basis of this obligation of the individual to the group, which represents a social commitment to mutual solidarity and security. The individual must contribute whatever resources he or she has available (be it labor power or a means of production) in order to remain within the collective. In the piecework atelier, for example, profit is accrued in the unequal movement of money between those doing the labor and those owning the means of production. But this unequal remuneration is seen to be lawful profit because it is based on a social agreement between the parties, rather than on the coercion of the marketplace.

The coercion of the marketplace *is* involved, of course, just as the owner's profit is a form of extraction of surplus value. The marketplace impinges by creating the class context for small-scale production. Formal-sector wages are depressed and inflation is high, creating a need for women's income but also a greater dependence on group solidarity and security. This dependence creates the ideological context for women's income production.

Large-scale rural-urban migration (also a result of economic forces and government economic policies that neglect the agricultural sector) provides an enormous pool of potential pieceworkers, depressing the piecework wage. Within this pool, women and atelier owners carve out stable production groups by means of a social agreement based on collective reciprocity which obligates the owner to give work to certain women first and the women to provide labor to the owner at little cost. This provides ready labor and stable quality for the owner and assured access to income for certain women. Government economic policies and their effect on the market prohibit expansion of small businesses into marketing and sales, forcing them to continue to rely on collective reciprocity for extraction of profit within the group. These conditions are advantageous to market forces outside of the group. Labor extracted through collective reciprocity fills the gap left by public- and private-sector wages that are below the subsistence level. The women's attitude toward labor as "not work," reinforced by the attitudes of intermediaries and merchants, lowers production costs and increases profits for the exporter and, ultimately, for the purveyor abroad of the goods made in this way.

Within the ideology of the traditional family, work for the production of surplus value is masked as labor expressing social and gender identity. Within the small commodity-producing group, individual acquisition, which is at the base of capitalist economic enterprise, coexists with reciprocal relations, which are at the base of long-term reproduction of Turkish social life.

Capitalist transactions (involving money) are embedded within and transformed by the cultural logic of the web of reciprocal indebtedness, which I have argued is the salient metaphor for social and economic life in Istanbul squatter districts. Within the specific cultural logic of small-scale commodity production in urban Turkey, relations of production are kinship relations. Not only is the expression of social identity also a form of capitalist production, but capitalist profit is morally just social profit, and economic exchange—or, from another point of view, labor exploitation—can be a means to social solidarity.

A shopkeeper chats with a friend.

Young girls in a workshop, punching holes in leather scraps. Since there are no men present, they have removed their headscarves.

Notes

1. Introduction

1. I use the word exploitation advisedly, since small-scale production does provide benefits to these women. Were they to work in a factory, they would perhaps gain a slightly higher wage and social benefits, but they would be backed into a different set of exploitative conditions. They would also lose the flexibility and social companionship of their commodity-producing environment.

2. Böhmer (1990) provides a detailed examination of Turkey's export policies between 1980 and 1987 along with a discussion of their political, economic, and cultural context.

3. See, for example, Benería and Roldán 1987, Bromley 1978, Harris 1978 and Moser 1978. Shelley Feldman (1991) examines the development of the informal-sector concept and compares it to other approaches to women's productive activities.

4. My research was conducted in a variety of neighborhoods which can be classified as squatter districts or as working-class neighborhoods. The boundaries of classification are no longer clear since both types of neighborhoods often contain legally as well as illegally built housing.

5. Kandiyoti questions studies that conclude that Turkish family roles "modernize" as a result of urbanization on the basis of such so-called emancipation factors as participation in mass media, greater freedom of movement, and role in decision making. "The problem with this and similar approaches . . . is that it gives little insight into the actual concrete dynamics of the situation. The same intricate mechanisms which link livelihood to family structure and attitudes continue to operate, even though the framework is more heterogeneous and complex" (1977:70).

6. For a recent discussion of the role of honor and shame in Mediterranean societies, see Gilmore 1987. For the role of children and childbearing in Turkey, see Kiray (1976), Kağıtçıbaşı (1982), and Delaney (1991a). In this book I concentrate primarily on the labor component of women's identity.

7. This idiom, which has generally been translated as "milk right," is

discussed in more detail in Chapter 5. In her discussion of breastfeeding in a Turkish village, where the practice is widespread and may continue up to the age of two, Carol Delaney suggests that milk rights represent a kind of "reciprocal feeding arrangement." "By depleting their own substance to substantiate a child, women establish *süt hakkı* (milk rights) to be supported and sustained by their grown children" (1991a:73).

8. In 1984 the wages of apprentices and unskilled workers in all sectors of small-scale industry in the city of Bursa were below minimum wage (Çinar, Evcimen, and Kaytaz 1988) as were the wages of Istanbul home workers in 1987 (Çinar 1989).

9. In June 1988 the Turkish newspaper *Cumhuriyet* estimated the minimum monthly expenditure for basic food items for a family of four living in Istanbul at 217,000 Turkish lira (TL), or about $146. The minimum wage was raised in 1988 so that the net monthly salary of the average worker was 83,000 TL ($56).

10. While systems of reciprocity work to the advantage of businesses, the roots of labor exploitation in Turkey lie deeper in particular structures of social and economic inequality. For example, income distribution in Istanbul has become polarized and class differences have intensified under the present government's liberal export-oriented economic policy. Likewise, worker's rights have been eroded by the repression of trade union activities.

11. This is a reflection of the complex and often contradictory relationship between Islam and secularism that characterizes Turkish society as a whole. For a discussion of this, see Yalman (1973), Heper (1981), and Mardin (1977).

12. See also Lordoğlu's study of pieceworkers in Bursa (1990).

13. Into this category are placed people who said that they had not been employed (*bir işte çalıştınız mı*), earning cash or in-kind income, during the previous week, but who answered positively to the question of whether they had worked (with the implication of 'on your own' or irregularly) (*bir iş yaptınız mı*), paid or unpaid, for even one hour during the same week. Both questions use the word *iş* (work), which many of the women in my study did not feel applied to them, even though they may have been doing piecework thirty or more hours a week.

14. This figure includes casual workers and unpaid family workers.

15. By this I do not mean that families are harmonious groups characterized by solidarity and a just distribution of resources. As will be seen in the following chapters, the family, like other social groups, is a complex site where vectors of power and resistance are acted out within certain naturalized ideological boundaries. Solidarity and dependence are but some of many possible practices.

16. This refers to increased decision-making opportunities regarding such things as choice of spouse, disposition of income, choice of consumer items, and spatial mobility. Further evidence that women's economic participation in small-scale production in various parts of the world fails to change their hierarchical position is given by Berik (1987, 1991), Benería & Roldán

(1987), Kuyaş (1982), Mies (1982, 1986), Abadan-Unat (1986:166), and Üşü-mezsoy (1993).

2. Bridge between Europe and Asia

1. The official figure given by the State Institute of Statistics is 150,000.

2. Rent-paying professionals have been known to express envy at the ability of more traditional families to build *gecekondu* housing. They themselves are unable to build such housing, although it would be an excellent investment, because, as they put it, "We would never be able to live in such an area." Class differences (and accompanying life-style differences) work against the financial interests of the middle classes in this case; however, it is generally known that wealthy people and large firms use migrants as their proxy, with an arrangement that when the land is legalized, ownership reverts to the sponsor. (Keleş [1983, pp. 211–212] discusses similar *gecekondu* speculation.)

3. Monthly rents for small apartments in *gecekondu* areas in 1988 began at 70,000 TL ($95).

4. While the ethnic homogeneity that had characterized many neighborhoods in the past has been replaced for the most part by class and income distinctions among areas of the city, individuals nevertheless still continue to orient themselves primarily by region of origin and membership in kinship groups.

5. *Ekonomik Panorama* 8/21/88, in an update of a 1973 study of income distribution in Istanbul by Süleyman Özmücür.

1973 monthly income categories (in TL): 0–999, 1,000–1,999, 2,000–2,999, 3,000–4,999, 5,000 +.
1987 (in thousand TL): 0–150, 150–400, 400–750, 750–1,500, 1,500 +.

The numerical content of the categories differs due to devaluation of the lira.

6. An exception to this is Zeytinburnu, the first *gecekondu* area in Istanbul. The movement of industry to that area contributed to further migrant settlement (*Yurt Ansiklopedisi* 1983:3999) and probably maintained its working-class characteristic.

3. Marriage: The House of the World

1. Twenty percent of marriages in Turkey are consanguineous, of which seven in ten are between first-degree relatives (cousins) (UNICEF 1991:253).

2. These regional and family ties may or may not coincide with residential proximity, although women who live near each other are more likely to visit each other frequently.

3. Kandiyoti (1988) gives a concise definition of this general concept, then goes on to discuss it within a comparative perspective.

4. Women in sub-Saharan Africa, for example, engage in trading activities which give them some autonomy in countering male attempts to control their labor and appropriate their production. This allows them to offset some of the insecurities of polygyny (Kandiyoti 1988).

5. One woman told me that her neighbors had asked her how she could allow a nonbeliever to stay in her house and to visit her so often. She said she told them that since I had a good heart, tried to keep the proper conventions, and expressed interest in Islam, that it was permissible.

6. By this is meant ongoing socialization throughout adult life, not only in childhood.

7. Sixty-three percent of marriages in villages are prearranged, compared to 19 percent in metropolitan areas (Timur 1972, cited in Abadan-Unat 1986:172). These figures, however, do not account for marriages in which parents set up meetings with potential marriage partners but the couple makes the final choice.

Oya Çitçi, in a study of female civil servants (reported in Abadan-Unat 1986:56), pointed out that only 10 percent of the women had acted completely independently in choosing their spouses, while 79.6 percent said that "they made their final decision after a harmonious consultation with their family" (Abadan-Unat 1986:56). Marriages arranged "in consultation with" the parents are often those among consanguineous relatives (first and second cousins).

8. During this meeting, the prospective bride serves small cups of Turkish coffee to the guests. If she likes her suitor, she serves him very sweet coffee. If she does not approve the match, she will serve him the coffee without sugar. No one else in the room will know of this communication, which allows the young man to save face by rejecting the match himself. Certain difficulties were encountered when, during the late 1970's, a shortage of foreign currency halted coffee imports and it was necessary to serve tea instead of coffee at the meetings between families. Tea is served in small tulip-shaped glasses, in which the amount of sugar is immediately visible. I observed this custom in Ankara in 1976, but I have not encountered it in Istanbul.

9. Specific grounds for divorce are: adultery, attempt on life, cruel treatment, infamous crime, dishonorable life, abandonment, insanity, and incompatibility (see Abadan-Unat 1986:177–180). Failure to provide financially for the family or infertility can be included in these categories.

10. Since religious marriages are not recognized by the state, neither the wife nor her children inherit if the husband dies. The children have difficulty obtaining personal documents and registering for school.

11. In a sense, however, usufruct of a home is shared with the husband's natal family.

12. A husband's decisions about his wife's access to her natal family may be influenced positively by his security in having complete access to her and therefore not feeling threatened. However, this presumes a careful juggling of time and responsibilities on the part of the wife *and* her mother.

13. Literally "the one who came." This is the term used to refer to the woman by her husband's family throughout her lifetime. She never becomes "the one who belongs." The terms "bride" or "wife" are insufficient translations of *gelin*, since they do not capture the implied sense of alienation and low hierarchical status.

14. It is not considered desirable for a man to live in his in-laws' household, or even in the same apartment building. A *gelin*, on the other hand, is moved as close as possible to her in-laws, often into the same apartment building if not the same physical household. Wealthy families, however, may build an apartment building and give an apartment to each of their children, including their daughters. Whether or not a married daughter lives in this apartment or rents it out and lives elsewhere depends to a great extent on the relative financial strength of her husband's family. If the apartment is rented out, the rent money, unlike a woman's gold, may be considered part of the family income and spent accordingly.

15. The groom's family traditionally pays for the wedding celebration, an expensive affair involving rental of a hall, with at least a piece of cake and a glass of lemonade for what may be a hundred or more guests and gifts of gold coins and money to be pinned on the couple. The groom's family is also expected to provide furniture (for the parlor and bedroom) as well as a previously negotiated number of gold bracelets, gold necklaces, and household items for the bride. The bride's family also has designated purchases and expenses, but these are usually not as high.

16. According to Turkish law in 1988, a married woman must have the permission of her husband to work outside the home. A man may terminate his wife's employment simply with a letter to the employer withdrawing his permission. This law has recently been rescinded.

17. Hiring a servant is not a solution, since the wife is still expected to devote all her time to supervising the work. One woman who worked full-time and paid the salary of a daily maid from her own pocket was the subject of angry attacks by her husband, who claimed she wasn't fulfilling her duty to him as wife, saying, "You don't even know where the salt is!" Service is not service unless it is personal. At issue also was what he considered her insufficient service to his natal family.

18. This is a common practice found even in working-class neighborhoods. The form of dwelling is smaller scale, but the principle is the same. The *gelin* spends much of her time in her mother-in-law's apartment. If the family is unable to build, they try to rent apartments for their sons in their own building.

19. Even in cases (such as the ones described above) in which a woman's family is able to keep her close by after her marriage, the amount of time and labor given by the bride to her natal family is a matter of careful balancing and negotiation. It must never interfere with the labor and time owed to her husband's family. Thus, proximity to her natal family often increases a woman's burden, at least in terms of labor and possible friction with her husband and his family.

In some cases, a woman's natal family did not offer shelter or moral support when she had a falling out with her husband; rather they sent her back
to her husband's house saying "that is where she belongs." This was most
often the position of the woman's father and was echoed by her mother
either out of fear of displeasing her husband or because she believed that
this is what was necessary to retain her daughter's marriage intact. Separation or divorce would bring shame and dishonor to both her daughter and
her own household.

20. It is beyond the scope of our discussion here, but it has been argued
that in certain respects the fundamental Islamic ethic protects a woman's
place *in the family* (cf. Coulson and Hinchcliffe 1978). While it is true
that some (but not all) very religious men in this study spend more time at
home with their families, this attention to the spirit and letter of Islam
usually also is accompanied by an intensification of restrictions on women's freedom of movement outside the home and their role in decision
making. I have heard of cases in which working-class women from conservative religious traditional families are not allowed out of the house at all
except under guidance of a husband (or mother-in-law), even in the case of
illness.

4. The Patriarch

1. It is said that when families go to view a prospective bride, they leave
some of the roasted chick-peas served them under the couch cushions. If at
the next visit the peas are still there, the girl is considered too untidy to be
a good wife. While this is not necessarily practiced, other things, such as
the girl's manner of serving coffee from a tray, are paid careful attention to.

2. Abadan-Unat (1986) writes that the custom of sons' taking care of
their parents may be changing, and that there is a trend for separate homes
for sons, with parents eventually living with the daughter and son-in-law.
Bolak (1991) confirms this, pointing out that, in practice, some women support their mothers better than their brothers. I did not encounter examples
of this type of household arrangement during my research. Most of the
women I spoke to still perceived their sons to be the basis of their future
security and well-being.

3. Such family dynamics are not unique to Turkish society. Patriarchal
family relations have been common in Europe and the United States until
recent times (cf. Boxer and Quataert 1987). They are still reflected in our
religious customs. Catholics, for example, pray to the Mother Mary to intercede for them with God the Father through her son Jesus (who through
the mystery of the Holy Trinity is one with God the Father). Note also the
centrality of the Mother Mary–son Jesus relationship in Catholic theology,
the relative unimportance and consequent impression of emotional distance of Joseph, Jesus' earthly father, and Jesus' petitioning of God the Father on the Mount of Olives and subsequent acceptance of God's will over
his own wishes.

4. Also means "spoiled," as in a spoiled child. The image is of a merry, carefree young girl.

5. While the explanation given for removing a girl from school is usually the one stated above, closer examination of the family situation and the girls' activities after leaving school shows that their labor was also needed, either at home to watch younger siblings while their mother worked, in a workshop, or for paid labor such as piecework, cleaning, or child care.

6. In a traditional family, if an unmarried girl is reported to have been alone in a room with an unrelated man, or even if she is seen on the street talking to a man, it might be difficult for her to find a husband because her virginity could be doubted. These prohibitions are somewhat more relaxed among less devout families, but virginity is still insisted upon.

Some families require a doctor's "virginity report" from a prospective bride if there are such rumors about her. The matter is taken very seriously. Doctors are loath to issue false reports because of the possibility of becoming involved in a lawsuit, should the deception be discovered. However, insistence upon a virginity report could be considered an insult to the honor of the girl's family and cause for stopping the marriage plans.

Virginity is still expected in a bride even among the most Westernized sectors of the community. One friend expressed her dilemma as her daughter approached her eighteenth birthday: "I raised my daughter in a completely Western, liberal way. Now how do I tell her that if she doesn't remain a virgin, it'll be next to impossible for her ever to marry a Turkish man?!"

7. Harris and Young (1981), in a classic article that deconstructs gender as a unified subject into empirical categories of relationships, distinguish among three kinds of reproduction: the reproduction of the social system, the reproduction of adequately socialized, adequately nourished labor (or of "adequate bearers of specific social relationships," that is, of nonlaborers), which I call here material reproduction, and specific forms of biological reproduction (1981:113). Women take a clear and significant place in all of these types of reproduction.

8. See Delaney (1991b) for a detailed discussion of the gender-based ideology of the Turkish state. According to Delaney, the terms "mother" and "father" have a specific meaning prior to their expression as roles, a meaning derived from a particular theory of procreation in which man is the creative agent and woman the nurturant medium. These definitions of male and female parenting are also projected onto power structures outside the family.

9. These examples were taken from newspaper accounts.

10. The United States also has a work ethic, an ideological motivation for labor, but one that is unique to our own culture and which emphasizes a profit motive over duty and reciprocity.

5. Mothers and Sons

1. The term "macho" is Turkish slang and has the same meaning as in English usage.

2. See Kononov (1956). According to Kononov, the Turkic word *oğ* means "tribe" and is related to *ög*, "mother." Sevortjan (1974) gives a probable meaning of the verb *oğ* as "to give birth to."

3. The lack of importance of the birth of girls is illustrated by the following story told to me by a man born in a town near Ankara. Ten or fifteen years ago, the town birth registry office burned in a fire. The town reregistered all men who had been born there, but none of the women.

4. Since Istanbul is a city of migrants from all parts of Turkey, such customs may vary from family to family.

5. Putting children to sleep earlier than the parents is structurally impossible in many working-class households where the children sleep in the sitting room on couch beds or on mattresses on the floor.

6. There is great variation in this pattern among different families and social classes, particularly with regard to the toleration of physical violence; nevertheless, I have encountered examples of such behavior in every class. Violence and social acceptance of violence, particularly against women, are also important and problematic aspects of U.S. society. However, it is important to understand how such behavior and attitudes interact with other elements of a particular cultural milieu.

7. This term generally has been translated as "milk right." The term *hak*, however, as it is used in other related verbal formulas (see Chapter 6) has the meaning of moral debt.

8. I did not observe this behavior in other homes, but I also did not stay with another family of this class (working class) and type (migrant, traditional but not conservative religious) that had a young son. However, other Turkish friends have observed similar behavior in working-class homes. Also, cartoons showing this same behavior with mothers and female guests appear occasionally in the major satirical magazine *Gırgır*, and I assume from that that the practice is common enough to be recognized by the readership.

9. With the spread of private Western-style bathrooms (with bathtub) in middle- and upper-class homes, bathing at a *hamam* has increasingly become a working-class activity. Most urban, middle-aged, middle-class women have never been to a *hamam*. The reasons given range from modesty about public nakedness to a belief that the *hamam* is dirty, or even to a fear of lesbian activity. Many working-class women, on the other hand, look forward to the *hamam* visit as a chance to relax and socialize. Historically, all classes have enjoyed the *hamam*; it was a center of social activity even for the Ottoman upper classes and the court.

The attitudes of middle-class women today toward the *hamam* seem to indicate the development of a sense of privacy and modesty, and a connection of female nakedness per se (not as seen through male eyes) with illicit sex, as well as to reflect a sense of distrust between classes. It is perhaps too soon to speculate on the effect of this middle-class modesty (prudery?) on the sexual education of young boys.

10. The range of male informants with whom I could discuss this was limited to several good friends, middle-class professionals. However, their explanations fit with the general tenor of male interaction that I have observed in Turkey and with published accounts of expected male attitudes and behavior toward women in the Middle East (see, for example, Mernissi 1975, and Abu-Lughod 1986). Individual behavior is affected by such matters as personality, social class, and educational background. However, normative patterns set the frame within which individual variation occurs. This discussion attempts to identify sets of expectations about certain types of behavior.

11. Delaney (1991a) also found little evidence in the Turkish village she studied that women had any knowledge of orgasm or masturbation, although some said they enjoyed sex. As Delaney points out, sexual practices is an area about which it is difficult to obtain accurate information or to generalize. Much of this discussion of the dynamics of sex and emotion among mother, son, and son's wife, therefore, is in the realm of conjecture, based on my own observations and discussions, but also informed by other published materials.

12. Housekeeping in a typical Turkish household involves continuous labor, especially in the winter because of the ubiquitous mud and seeping coal dust from the heating systems. Electric household appliances are not common. Floors and carpets are swept and washed by hand; clothes are often washed by hand, although electric washers have become more common in middle-class homes. Traditional Turkish cooking is also labor-intensive and time-consuming. A series of different dishes is prepared for each meal, the contents varying according to the family budget.

6. The Social Web

1. In Turkey grinding poverty, untrammeled exploitation of labor, early aging, and death coexist with an unshakable sense of security and well-being associated with membership in a family and group. Turkey's famous "guest-friendliness" (*misafirperverlik*) derives from this obligation of the group to take care of the individual.

2. At that time, 50 TL was a substantial enough amount to expect it in change. As a result of continuous devaluation, 50 TL no longer exists as a denomination, the lowest coin being 100 TL.

3. *Süt hakkı* generally has been translated as "milk right." However, in light of the following discussion of use of the word *hak* in the ritual forgiving of moral debts, I believe that the meaning of the term *süt hakkı* implies a moral debt. I have preferred to translate it as "milk debt" in order to make this meaning clearer.

4. While daily purchases from the ubiquitous small neighborhood grocery stores can be paid for in cash, most business is done on credit.

5. Naked economic domination and exploitation are present, for example, in factories. However, while such domination may be said to occur at the level of abstraction of worker/capitalist, I would argue that the individual worker and the individual representative of the capitalist (e.g., the foreman) interact *whenever possible* as nodes within the social web. Workers, for example, often obtain their jobs through friends (or more distant connections) who already work at the factory.

6. The limitation of the practice of power in Turkey to the possibilities inherent in the web metaphor helps explain the inability of Western feminist thought, based on the concept of individual power and autonomy, to make more than superficial inroads into the Turkish discourse of power, despite the attempts of a vocal minority of educated feminist Turkish women. It is, rather, the discourse of conservative Islamic thought that is currently gaining the upper hand in the ongoing battle to define Turkish social and national identity. While it is beyond the scope of this book, it would be interesting to reflect on the construction of power in the ideology of various increasingly important Islamic groups in Turkey.

7. Money Makes Us Relatives

1. This depends on the product. Clothing and knitted goods in particular are exported.

2. There have been attempts to go beyond spatial and coresidential criteria in defining households. See, for example, Smith, Wallerstein, and Evers (1984) and the work of Sylvia Yanagisako (1979).

3. I will refer to the business as atelier and to the physical location of production as workshop. This distinction becomes important when discussing changes in the physical and functional arrangement of the atelier.

4. I use this term advisedly, since knitting, crocheting, embroidery, and other "traditional" women's activities do require skill and many years of training. Use of the term "unskilled labor" to refer to squatter residents by researchers itself constitutes a devaluation of women's "traditional" activities as being unsuited to the capitalist labor market. This is patently a myth that reinforces the social valuation of these women's labor as a leisure activity.

5. Conversions reflect differences in the exchange rate during the fieldwork period.

6. About $47, slightly below the official minimum wage.

7. Although the purchase of such an expensive machine may seem a risky economic decision, I believe the knitting machine is merely an updated version of the sewing machine, a traditional purchase for the household. The important similarity is that these machines are purchased primarily to produce clothing for one's own family, thereby saving money, even if other items also are produced for sale. Like household furniture, the ma-

chines are not a business investment, and risk is not a factor taken into account.

8. In September 1988 the official rate of inflation approached 80 percent, but actual inflation for staple food products (between 7/87 and 7/88) ranged from 150 percent (for bread) to 430 percent (for rice).

9. In Turkey the yarn is passed around the back of the neck before it is worked with the knitting needles. This makes it easier for women to knit while standing or even walking.

10. The labor force participation rate for urban women fell even lower to 15.2 percent by 1990, despite the fact that there was a 2.3 percent decline in unemployment for this population during that time. The rate for men fell also between 1988 and 1990, from 72.9 to 70.3 percent, along with a 1 percent rise in the urban male unemployment rate. The overall unemployment rate for the urban population remained stable, rising by only .2 percent during this period (SIS 1990b).

11. A former (1950) prime minister of Turkey.

12. A downtown business and garment district.

13. The exchange rate changed rapidly during the fieldwork period. The dollar equivalents given reflect these variations.

14. Çinar (1989:19–20) also notes that although subcontracting (piecework) wages in Istanbul and Bursa were at a par with the gross formal-sector minimum wage, when the minimum wage was raised there was no corresponding increase in subcontracting wages. This discrepancy is exacerbated by the fact that formal-sector employment also provides health, pregnancy, vacation, and retirement benefits which are not available in home employment.

15. *İmece* means work done for the community by the entire village or by the united efforts of the community (*Redhouse* 1983, s.v. "imece"). In a broader sense, however, the word means work done as enduring, collective (*ortaklaşa*) reciprocal assistance (*karşılıklı yardımlaşma*) (cf. Eyuboğlu 1988).

16. *Bedelsiz* means without equivalent value expected in exchange.

17. The *Redhouse* dictionary (1983) defines *ırgat* as day laborer or workman. Eyuboğlu (1988) gives the Anatolian usage of the word as a worker who subsists on agriculture. In the context in which it is used by Osman, it may mean agricultural labor to meet a social or financial obligation or perhaps agricultural labor given with no return.

18. His daughter Emine's teenage friend whom I had seen on various visits punching holes in leather pieces. Later in the year, as production increased in response to larger orders, she began to work in the atelier regularly and received a small wage.

19. Peddlers sell their wares, usually household goods, on an installment plan, passing through a neighborhood at regular intervals to pick up payment.

20. He uses 100 percent cotton yarn that is custom dyed by a small firm.

21. Since 1980 the Turkish government has encouraged exports through generous credits and subsidies.

22. Berik (1987:3) describes a similar attitude among Turkish women carpet weavers in rural Turkey who regard weaving as "an integral part of their
lives as 'peasants,' farmers and women, and do not consider themselves as
'workers.'" Carpet weaving in the home is interpreted by the community
and by the weavers themselves as a leisure activity, even though it may be
a full-time activity.

8. The Life Cycle of an Atelier: Yenikent

1. As opposed to making in order to sell.
2. About $7,000. This seems a bit high, but I was not able to verify the
amount with Murad.
3. While this may seem an extreme case, I have in fact heard of such
refused opportunities in other ateliers. A related phenomenon occurs when
an atelier owner takes on a large order that is to be exported but is negligent
about the quality of production (in one case, the owner neglected to be present during a critical phase of production) so that, after a few orders, the
contract is withdrawn.
4. Kuşadası is a tourist resort on the Aegean coast near Izmir.
5. The inflation rate for 1987–1988 was around 70 percent and the price
of yarn rose quickly.
6. While piecework ateliers have a different context for reinvestment and
expansion than businesses outside the community that use piecework labor
as only a part of their production process, in some cases these businesses do
exhibit a similar aversion to risk. For example, Ahmet's stationery supply
wholesale business has an office, a fax machine, and two full-time employees. Nevertheless, he orders supplies and has materials processed in cautious amounts that reflect his orders, so that there is little excess in his
storeroom. If he is able to obtain an export contract with Saudi Arabia, that
will be the impetus for increasing production.

9. Kinship and Capitalism

1. See, for example, the overview of Marxist-feminist analysis by Barrett
(1980), Mies (1986b), and Redclift (1988). Alison Scott (1986), in her review
of the literature on petty commodity production, also makes this observation. A recent interesting analysis by Winnie Lem (1991) rethinks the concepts of family and household in order to better approach issues of ideology
and power in petty commodity production in southern France.
2. Since the differences between specific terminologies used in Marxist
and neo-Marxist analyses of this type of production are not directly relevant to my discussion and may be confusing to the general reader, I have
preferred to use the more general term small-scale commodity production or, more simply, small-scale production. The terms petty commodity
production and simple commodity production, for example, refer to different parameters of small-scale production within Marxist economic theory.
Simple commodity production, a term formulated by Friedmann (1980),

for example, differentiates a type of small-scale production specific to capitalism.

3. Lower-class women in the informal sector, writes Moore (1988), engage in the capitalist economy "in a way which does not depend on a rigid separation of the 'home' from the 'workplace', . . . managing the domestic labour of the household as well as earning a living. They are neither housewives nor wage labourers, and as such Marxist-feminist analysis has very little to say about them" (91).

4. In discussing the literature on relations between capitalism and the family, Friedmann reports different authors as concluding that families and marriage are, in some sense, "relations of production" (1986:50, 53) but clearly does not mean this in the Marxist sense. Nevertheless, the direction of her comments is provocative.

5. By this is meant the transformation of private property into social property.

References

Abadan-Unat, Nermin
  1986 *Women in the Developing World: Evidence from Turkey.* Denver: University of Denver Press.
Abu-Lughod, Lila
  1986 *Veiled Sentiments: Honor and Poetry in a Bedouin Society.* Berkeley: University of California Press.
Bang, W.
  1918 Zu den Wörtern auf *-turuq, -duq. Túrán,* no. 5.
Barrett, M.
  1980 *Women's Oppression Today: Problems in Marxist Feminist Analysis.* London: Verso.
Baud, Isa
  1987 Industrial Subcontracting: The Effects of the Putting Out System on Poor Working Women in India. In *Invisible Hands,* ed. Singh and Kelles-Viitanen, pp. 69–91.
Beck, L., and N. Keddie, eds.
  1978 *Women in the Muslim World.* Cambridge: Harvard University Press.
Benería, Lourdes
  1979 Reproduction, Production, and the Sexual Division of Labor. *Cambridge Journal of Economics* 3:203–225.
Benería, Lourdes, and Martha Roldán
  1987 *The Crossroads of Class and Gender: Industrial Homework, Subcontracting, and Household Dynamics in Mexico City.* Chicago: University of Chicago Press.
Berik, Günseli
  1987 *Women Carpet Weavers in Rural Turkey: Patterns of Employment, Earnings, and Status.* Geneva: International Labour Office.
  1991 Zur gesellschaftlichen Lage von Teppichknüpferinnen: Formen weiblicher Unterdrückung und Struktur ländlich-industrieller und landwirtschaftlicher Tätigkeit. In *Aufstand im Haus der Frauen,* ed. Neusel, Tekeli, and Akkent, pp. 149–163.

Bernstein, Henry
  1986   Capitalism and Petty Commodity Production. *Social Analysis* 20: 11–28.
Böhmer, Jochen
  1990   *Zwischen Exportboom und Re-Islamisierung: Stabilisierungs-und Strukturanpassungspolitik in der Türkei 1980–1987.* Hamburg: Lit Verlag.
Bolak, Hale
  1991   Wenn die Frau das Geld verdient . . . : Machtverhältnisse in Städtischen Arbeiterfamilien. In *Aufstand im Haus der Frauen,* ed. Neusel, Tekeli, and Akkent, pp. 229–241.
Borie, Alain, Pierre Pinon, Stephane Yerasimos, and Attila Yücel
  1987   Istanbul. *Mimar* 12/26.
Bottomore, Tom, ed.
  1983   *A Dictionary of Marxist Thought.* Cambridge: Harvard University Press.
Bourdieu, Pierre
  1979   *Outline of a Theory of Practice.* London: Cambridge University Press.
Boxer, Marilyn J., and Jean H. Quataert
  1987   *Connecting Spheres: Women in the Western World, 1500 to the Present.* Oxford: Oxford University Press.
Boysan, A., and B. Boysan
  1987   Yeditepe'den 57 Tepeye. *Hürriyet,* May 18, p. 5.
Brass, Tom
  1986   The Elementary Structures of Kinship: Unfree Relations and the Production of Commodities. *Social Analysis* 20: 56–68.
Bromley, Ray
  1978   Introduction—The Urban Informal Sector: Why Is It Worth Discussing? *World Development* 6 (9/10): 1033–1039.
Bromley, Ray, and Chris Gerry
  1979   *Casual Work and Poverty in Third World Cities.* New York: John Wiley and Sons.
Chevalier, Jacques M.
  1983   There is Nothing Simple about Simple Commodity Production. *Journal of Peasant Studies* 10 (4): 153–186.
Çinar, E. Mine
  1989   Taking Work at Home: Disguised Female Employment in Urban Turkey. Loyola University of Chicago School of Business Administration Working Paper No. 8810. Chicago: Loyola University.
  1991   Labor Opportunities for Adult Females and Home-Working Women in Istanbul, Turkey. Los Angeles: University of California, The G. E. von Grunebaum Center for Near Eastern Studies.
Çinar, E. Mine, Günar Evcimen, and Mehmet Kaytaz
  1985   The Potential Growth of Small Scale Industries in Less Developed Countries: The Case of Turkey. Paper presented at Middle East Studies Association Annual Meeting.

1988   The Present Day Status of Small-Scale Industries (Sanatkar) in Bursa, Turkey. *International Journal of Middle East Studies* 20 (3): 287–301.

Cohen, M.
1988   *Women's Work, Markets, and Economic Development in Nine-teenth-Century Ontario.* Toronto: University of Toronto Press.

Coulson, Noel, and Doreen Hinchcliffe
1978   Women and Law Reform in Contemporary Islam. In *Women in the Muslim World,* edited by Lois Beck and N. Keddie, pp. 37–51. Cambridge: Harvard University Press.

Delaney, Carol
1987   Seeds of Honor, Fields of Shame. In *Honor and Shame and the Unity of the Mediterranean,* ed. Gilmore, pp. 35–48.
1991a   *The Seed and the Soil: Gender and Cosmology in Turkish Village Society.* Berkeley: University of California Press.
1991b   Father State (Devlet Baba), Motherland (Anavatan), and the Birth of Modern Turkey. Paper presented at the American Ethnological Society Meetings, Spring 1991.

Diamond, Norma
1975   Collectivization, Kinship, and the Status of Women in Rural China. In *Toward an Anthropology of Women,* ed. Reiter, pp. 372–395.

Duben, Alan
1982   The Significance of Family and Kinship in Urban Turkey. In *Sex Roles, Family, and Community in Turkey,* ed. Kağıtçıbaşı, pp. 73–100.
1990   Household Formation in Late Ottoman Istanbul. *International Journal of Middle East Studies* 22 (4): 419–435.

Durrenberger, E. Paul
1980   Chayanov's Economic Analysis in Anthropology. *Journal of Anthropological Research* 36 (2): 133–148.

Eyuboğlu, Ismet Zeki
1988   *Türk Dilinin Etimoloji Sözlüğü.* Istanbul: Sosyal Yayınlar.

Feldman, Shelley
1991   Still Invisible: Women in the Informal Sector. *Women and International Development Annual,* Volume 2. Boulder: Westview Press.

Friedman, Kathie
1984   Households as Income-Pooling Units. In *Households and the World-Economy,* ed. Smith, Wallerstein, and Evers, pp. 37–55.

Friedmann, Harriet
1980   Household Production and the National Economy: Concepts for the Analysis of Agrarian Formations. *Journal of Peasant Studies* 7:158–184.
1986   Patriarchal Commodity Production. *Social Analysis* 20:47–55.
1987   The Family Farm and the International Food Regimes. In *Peasants*

and Peasant Societies, edited by Teodor Shanin. Oxford: Basil Blackwell.

Gibbon, P., and M. Neocosmos
1985   Some Problems in the Political Economy of "African Socialism." In *Contradictions of Accumulation in Africa: Studies in Economy and State*, edited by H. Bernstein and B. K. Campbell. Beverly Hills: Sage.

Gilmore, David D., ed.
1987   *Honor and Shame and the Unity of the Mediterranean*. Washington: American Anthropological Association.

Godelier, Maurice
1988   *The Mental and the Material*. London: Verso.

Hacettepe University
1989   *1988 Turkish Population and Health Survey*. Ankara: Institute of Population Studies.

Harris, Olivia, and K. Young
1981   Engendered Structures: Some Problems in the Analysis of Reproduction. In *The Anthropology of Pre-Capitalist Societies*, edited by Joel Kahn and J. R. Llobera, pp. 109–147. Atlantic Highlands, N.J.: Humanities Press.

Harris, Barbara
1978   Quasi-Formal Employment Structures and Behaviour in the Unorganized Urban Economy, and the Reverse: Some Evidence from South India. *World Development* 6 (9/10): 1077–1086.

Heper, Metin
1981   Islam, Polity, and Society in Turkey: A Middle Eastern Perspective. *Middle East Journal* 35:345–363.

Joseph, Suad
1978   Women and the Neighborhood Street in Borj Hammoud, Lebanon. In *Women in the Muslim World*, ed. Beck and Keddie, pp. 541–557.

Kağıtçıbaşı, Çiğdem
1982   Sex Roles, Value of Children and Fertility. In *Sex Roles, Family, and Community in Turkey*, edited by Ciğdem Kağıtçıbaşı, pp. 151–180. Bloomington: Indiana University Turkish Studies.

Kahn, Joel S.
1978   Marxist Anthropology and Peasant Economics: A Study of the Social Structures of Underdevelopment. In *The New Economic Anthropology*, edited by John Clammer, pp. 110–137. New York: St. Martin's Press.

1980   *Minangkabau Social Formations*. Cambridge: Cambridge University Press.

Kandiyoti, Deniz
1977   Sex Roles and Social Change: A Comparative Appraisal of Turkey's Women. *Signs: A Journal of Women in Culture and Society* 3 (1): 57–73.

1988   Bargaining with Patriarchy. *Gender and Society* 2 (3): 274–290.

Kartal, Kemal
1978   *Kentleşme Ve İnsan.* Ankara: Türkiye ve Orta Doğu Amme İdaresi Enstitüsü.
Kayır, Arşalus
1991   Zu sexuellen Problemen von Frauen. In *Aufstand im Haus der Frauen,* ed. Neusel, Tekeli, and Akkent, pp. 298–312.
Keleş, Ruşen
1983   *100 Soruda Türkiye'de Kentleşme, Konut ve Gecekondu.* (1972) Istanbul: Gerçek Yayinevi.
Keleş, Ruşen, and Geoffrey Payne
1984   Turkey. In *Planning and Urban Growth in Southern Europe,* edited by Martin Wynn, pp. 165–197. London: Mansell.
Kiray, Mübeccel
1976   The New Role of Mothers: Changing Intra-Familial Relationships in a Small Town in Turkey. In *Mediterranean Family Structures,* edited by J. G. Peristiany, pp. 261–271. Cambridge: Cambridge University Press.
Kononov, A.
1956   K ètimologii slova *oyul* 'syn.' In *Filologija i istorija mongolskich narodov.* Moscow.
Kuyaş, Nilüfer
1982   Female Labor Power Relations in the Urban Turkish Family. In *Sex Roles, Family, and Community in Turkey,* ed. Kağıtçıbaşı, pp. 181–206.
Lem, Winnie
1991   Gender, Ideology, and Petty Commodity Production: Social Reproduction in Languedoc, France. In *Marxist Approaches in Economic Anthropology,* edited by A. Littlefield and H. Gates, pp. 103–117. Lanham, Md.: University Press of America.
Levine, Ned
1982   Social change and family crisis—the nature of Turkish divorce. In *Sex Roles, Family, and Community in Turkey,* ed. Kağıtçıbaşı, pp. 151–180.
Long, Norman, and Paul Richardson
1978   Informal Sector, Petty Commodity Production, and the Social Relations of Small-Scale Enterprise. In *New Economic Anthropology,* ed. Clammer, pp. 176–209.
Lordoğlu, Kuvvet
1990   Eve İş Verme Sistemi İçinde Kadın İşgücü Üzerine Bir Alan Araştırması. Istanbul: Friedrich Ebert Vakfı.
Mardin, Şerif
1977   Religion in Modern Turkey. *International Social Science Journal* 29 (2): 279–297.
Marx, Karl
1971   *The Grundrisse.* New York: Harper & Row.

Mauss, Marcel
   1967   *The Gift.* New York: W. W. Norton.
Meeker, Michael E.
   1976   Meaning and Society in the Near East: Examples from the Black
          Sea Turks and the Levantine Arabs (Part 2). *International Journal
          of Middle East Studies* 7:383–422.
Mernissi, Fatima
   1975   *Beyond the Veil: Male-Female Dynamics in a Modern Muslim So-
          ciety.* New York: John Wiley and Sons.
el-Messiri, Sawsan
   1978   Self-Images of Traditional Urban Women in Cairo. In *Women in
          the Muslim World,* ed. Beck and Keddie, pp. 522–540.
Mies, Maria
   1982   *The Lace Makers of Narsapur: Indian Housewives Produce for the
          World Market.* London: Zed Press.
   1986a *Indian Women in Subsistence and Agricultural Labour.* Geneva:
          International Labour Office.
   1986b *Patriarchy and Accumulation on a World Scale.* London: Zed
          Press.
Mies, M., V. Bennholdt-Thomsen, and C. von Werlhof, eds.
   1988   *Women: The Last Colony.* London: Zed Books.
Miles Doan, Rebecca
   1992   Class Differentiation and the Informal Sector in Amman, Jordan.
          International Journal of Middle East Studies 24:27–38.
Moore, Henrietta L.
   1988   *Feminism and Anthropology.* Cambridge: Polity Press.
Moser, Caroline O. N.
   1978   Informal Sector or Petty Commodity Production: Dualism or De-
          pendence in Urban Development? *World Development* 6 (9/10):
          1041–1064.
Neusel, Aylâ, Şirin Tekeli, and Meral Akkent, eds.
   1991   *Aufstand im Haus der Frauen: Frauenforschung aus der Türkei.*
          Berlin: Orlanda Frauenverlag.
Olson, Emilie A.
   1982   Duofocal Family Structure and an Alternative Model of Husband-
          Wife Relationships. In *Sex Roles, Family, and Community in Tur-
          key,* ed. Kağıtçıbaşı, pp. 33–72.
Özbay, Ferhunde
   1982   Women's Education in Rural Turkey. In *Sex Roles, Family, and
          Community in Turkey,* ed. Kağıtçıbaşı, pp. 151–180.
   1991a Türkiye'de Kadın ve Çocuk Emeği. *Toplum ve Bilim* 53:41–54.
   1991b Der Wandel der Arbeitssituation der Frau in innerhäuslichen
          und ausserhäuslichen Bereich in den letzten sechzig Jahren. In
          Aufstand im Haus der Frauen, ed. Neusel, Tekeli, and Akkent,
          pp. 120–148.

Parry, Jonathan, and Maurice Bloch, eds.
1989 *Money and the Morality of Exchange.* Cambridge: Cambridge University Press.

Redclift, Nanneke
1988 Gender, Accumulation, and the Labour Process. In *On Work*, edited by R. E. Pahl, pp. 428–448. Oxford: Basil Blackwell.

Redhouse Turkish-English Dictionary
1983 Istanbul: Redhouse Press.

Reiter, Rayna R., ed.
1975 *Toward an Anthropology of Women.* New York: Monthly Review Press.

Roldán, Martha
1985 Industrial Outworking, Struggles for the Reproduction of Working-Class Families, and Gender Subordination. In *Beyond Employment: Household, Gender, and Subsistence*, edited by Nanneke Redclift and E. Mingione, pp. 248–285. New York: Basil Blackwell.

Rosaldo, Michelle Zimbalist, and Louise Lamphere
1974 *Woman, Culture, and Society.* Stanford: Stanford University Press.

Rosen, Lawrence
1978 The Negotiation of Reality: Male-Female Relations in Sefrou, Morocco. In *Women in the Muslim World*, ed. Beck and Keddie, pp. 561–584.

Scott, Alison MacEwen
1979 Who Are the Self-Employed? In *Casual Work and Poverty*, ed. Bromley and Gerry, pp. 105–129.
1986 Introduction: Why Rethink Petty Commodity Production? *Social Analysis* 20: 3–10.

Scott, James
1985 *Weapons of the Weak: Everyday Forms of Peasant Resistance.* New Haven: Yale University Press.

Şenyapılı, Tansı
1981 *Gecekondu: Çevre İşçilerin Mekanı.* Ankara: Middle East Technical University Department of Architecture.

Sevortjan, È. V.
1974 Ètimologičeskij slovar' tjurkskich jazykov. Band 1, pp. 414–417.

Singh, Andrea Menefee, and Anita Kelles-Viitanen
1987 Introduction. In *Invisible Hands: Women in Home-Based Production*, edited by A. M. Singh and A. Kelles-Viitanen, pp. 13–26. New Delhi: Sage.

SIS (Turkish State Institute of Statistics)
1980, 1990a *Survey of Industry.*
1990b *Household Labor Force Survey Results.*

Smith, Carol A.
1984a Does a Commodity Economy Enrich the Few While Ruining the Masses? Differentiation among Petty Commodity Producers in Guatemala. *Journal of Peasant Studies* 11 (3): 60–95.

1984b Forms of Production in Practice: Fresh Approaches to Simple Commodity Production. *Journal of Peasant Studies* 11 (4): 201–221.
1986 Reconstructing the Elements of Petty Commodity Production. *Social Analysis* 20:29–46.

Smith, Joan, I. Wallerstein, and H.-D. Evers, eds.
1984 *Households and the World-Economy*. Beverly Hills: Sage.

Tümertekin, Erol
1973 *Urbanization and Urban Functions in Turkey*. Istanbul: Istanbul University Geographical Institute.

Tümertekin, Erol, and Nazmiye Özgüç
1977 *Distribution of Out-Born Population in Istanbul: Case Study on Migration*. Istanbul: Çağlayan.

UNFPA (United Nations Fund for Population Activities)
1986 *Giant Cities of the World*. Barcelona: Corporació Metropolitana de Barcelona.

UNICEF and Government of Turkey
1991 *The Situation Analysis of Mothers and Children in Turkey*. Ankara: UNICEF.

UNIDO (United Nations Industrial Development Fund) and Islamic Conference Organization SESRTCIC (Statistical, Economic, and Social Research and Training Centre for Islamic Countries)
1987 *Small and Medium Sized Manufacturing Enterprises in Turkey*.

Üşümezsoy, Belkıs
1993 Women's Informal-Sector Contribution to Household Survival in Urban Turkey. Istanbul: Marmara University, Ph.D. dissertation.

Van Baal, J.
1975 *Reciprocity and the Position of Women*. Amsterdam: Van Gorcum, 1975.

Yalman, Nur
1973 Some Observations on Secularism in Islam: The Cultural Revolution in Turkey. *Daedalus* 102 (1973): 139–168.

Yanagisako, Sylvia Junko
1979 Family and Household: The Analysis of Domestic Groups. *Annual Review of Anthropology* 8:161–205.

Yüksel, Şahika
1991 Körperliche Misshandlung in der Familie und die Solidaritätskampagne 'Gegen Gewalt an Frauen'. In *Aufstand im Haus der Frauen*, ed. Neusel, Tekeli, and Akkent, pp. 287–297.

Yurt Ansiklopedisi
1983 *Istanbul*. Istanbul: Anadolu Yayıncılık.

Index